FLEX EDUCATION

LINDSAY PATIENCE
AND LUCY ROSE

FLEX EDUCATION

A GUIDE FOR FLEXIBLE WORKING IN SCHOOLS

SAGE Publications Ltd
1 Oliver's Yard
55 City Road
London EC1Y 1SP

A SAGE company
2455 Teller Road
Thousand Oaks, California 91320
(0800)233-9936
www.corwin.com

SAGE Publications India Pvt Ltd
B 1/I 1 Mohan Cooperative Industrial Area
Mathura Road
New Delhi 110 044

SAGE Publications Asia-Pacific Pte Ltd
3 Church Street
#10-04 Samsung Hub
Singapore 049483

Editor: Diana Alves
Publisher: James Clark
Senior project editor: Chris Marke
Project management: TNQ Technologies
Marketing Manager: Dilhara Attygalle
Cover design: Wendy Scott
Typeset by: TNQ Technologies
Printed in the UK

First published in 2022

Library of Congress Control Number: 2021943735

British Library Cataloguing in Publication Data

A catalogue record for this book is available from the British Library.

ISBN 978-1-5297-4487-3
ISBN 978-1-5297-4486-6 (pbk)

CONTENTS

ABOUT THE AUTHORS

After studying Economics and Management at Jesus College, Oxford, **Lindsay Patience** trained to teach Business Studies and Economics through the Teach First programme. After 10 years working in schools as a teacher and senior leader, she found herself looking for a part-time leadership role in education after she had her first child. She was shocked to find that there were no roles available and struggled to find a part-time job even as a classroom teacher. When talking to others, she realised she was certainly not alone in this and began to hear more and more how limited flexible working opportunities were in schools. This came at a time when the recruitment and retention crisis in teaching was really starting to ramp up, and frustrated by the issue, she began a project with the Teach First Innovation Unit to research and develop solutions. This is where she met Lucy Rose, and their work really crystallised the link between the retention and wellbeing of teachers and the outcomes for pupils and how important flexible working was to improving these. She now works part-time as an Economics and Business teacher at a London secondary school.

Lucy Rose joined the Teach First programme in 2004 and trained as a teacher of Spanish and French. She shared the school journey from Special Measures to Outstanding working in a variety of roles as a middle and senior leader. After having her son, she was disappointed to find resistance to flexible working and a strong culture of presenteeism which was difficult to navigate. She left full-time teaching after her daughter was born and during this 'break', she retrained as an English specialist, became ridiculously interested in timetabling and met Lindsay at the Innovation Series. Lucy now works flexibly teaching English at a London secondary school.

ACKNOWLEDGEMENTS

Flexible Teacher Talent is an organisation which promotes flexible working in the education sector. We help individual teachers and school leaders who are working, or looking to work, flexibly and we support schools to introduce and embrace flexible working.

Lucy and Lindsay would like to thank all those flexing the system to make it work for them and the pupils they serve. Many of those living and breathing flexibility feature in this book, and we thank them for sharing their stories as a positive example to us all. We thank our patient editor Diana Alves and SAGE for believing in us and helping us to get this book finished.

Thank you to all those who did not blink when we appeared for meetings with babies and children and for the #WomenEd and #HeadsForward conferences which included a crèche so that CPD did not have to stop with maternity leave.

Thank you to our sister organisations the MTPTproject, ReturntoTeach and the Shared Headship Network as well as those in the #WomenEd network, especially Hannah Wilson, Angie Browne and Vivienne Porritt. Special thanks to Emma Sheppard and Holly Power who share our parental teaching journey from frustration to delight on an almost daily basis.

Lucy would like to thank her Mum who navigated part-time and worked flexibly, long before it was fashionable. She would like to thank her husband Tom who works flexibly, shares childcare and parenting equitably and has come up with more flex puns than anyone. She would also like to thank her children Jonah and Neve whose existence insisted that she demand another way of working.

Lindsay acknowledges all of those working flexibly in schools who are paving the way for future generations to have genuine choices about how they live and work. Thank you for the example you set and the battles you fight in order to make the path smoother for those who come after you. She hopes that the future will be fairer and more flexible for her children, Lucy and Rory.

1

FLEXIBLE WORKING IN SCHOOLS

In this chapter we will:

- Outline the current situation regarding flexible working in schools
- Consider the big picture need for change and flexibility in the education sector
- Give an overview of what this book is for and how it can be used

> *Ensuring there are enough high-quality teachers in England's schools is crucial for delivering a first-class education for young people. Attracting and retaining enough secondary teachers is a key challenge facing school leaders today. Providing more opportunities for part-time and flexible working may provide part of the answer.*
>
> (Sharp et al., 2019)

...Flexible and part-time working opportunities are increasingly important

> *[Teachers leaving the profession often move to flexible or part-time work – there appears to be unmet demand for part-time work in schools. Only 28% of female teachers work part-time, compared to an average of 40% of women in the UK and fewer men do too (8% compared to 12% in the whole economy). Improving opportunities to work flexibly will be important in retaining more teachers in the profession and in attracting returners and career changers.*
>
> (Department for Education, 2019)

Introduction

This book is designed to be used flexibly. Read in its entirety or choose specific chapters relevant to your context. We have shared our 'Why' in this chapter, but understand that many of you would rather just get right on with the more practical elements of the book.

We received the news from our editor that we could go ahead with this book just before the lockdown in March 2020. At the time, flexible and remote working were not commonplace in education and we were lagging about thirty years behind other industries. Our mission was to improve pupil outcomes by supporting schools and individuals to work more flexibly. At the time, and alongside our flexible teaching day jobs, that meant working with schools who wanted to use flexible working to recruit and retain teachers and running workshops with groups of individuals (mostly parents) who were interested in returning to work after an extended break. Lindsay and her newborn baby, Rory, attended focus groups at the Department for Education. We were encouraged and supported by #WomenEd, #DiverseEd and The Chartered College of Teaching to speak and run workshops at their conferences. We shared data, stories of excellent practice and offered e-mail support for individuals wanting advice on how to complete a flexible working request. We could see the landscape changing very gradually and we were grateful for the opportunity to extend our reach with this book because, for the most part, we were supporting individuals against a system which was not working for them. We advocated a rethink and a system which worked for everyone. The more we got into this work with schools and individuals, the more we were convinced that flexibility benefitted teachers, schools and pupils: the entire system.

It seems hard to imagine now that we were supporting so many teachers and school leaders who were dealing with rejections to flexible working requests because they would be 'unable to attend key meetings', 'miss out on whole staff CPD' or because there were 'concerns about staff being off site or leading remotely'. We were working with people who had been told that there was just 'no way' of attending briefings remotely while their school was fully signed up to a Microsoft package including Teams but no one used the software. It was a different time and we do not wish to be flippant about the COVID-19 pandemic, but it has to have some silver lining and in this 'new normal', these unsubstantiated arguments and out-of-hand rejections no longer seem acceptable. Overnight, much of what had been so often argued as 'impossible' was suddenly possible. This meant some of our initial ideas for the book changed, but watching schools suddenly adopt practices we had advocated should be available to everyone was worth it. Slow, gradual changes to the flexible working landscape in our sector were replaced with these rapid and immediate changes that look set to change the options available permanently. There were many challenges and misappropriations and misuse of the true meaning of 'flexible working' during this time but overall, the changes for flexibility in the sector will be positive.

In 2016, we met on a programme run by the TeachFirst Innovation unit which supported teachers and school leaders to address issues they had identified in the education sector. We had both been working full time as senior leaders in challenging urban complex schools and had identified issues with women either leaving teaching altogether or returning to less senior roles after maternity leave. We say 'identified', but we were also those women and we were living these issues ourselves. We wanted someone to take what we thought was our own problem seriously. We thought someone, somewhere should at least have created a job-share platform. Where was the support we needed? With a bit of a reading, we realised that there were 6,000 more of us each year who left the teaching profession (Department for Education, 2014). We loved our jobs and did not want to join that number. We advocate flexible opportunities for all, but at the time it was this haemorrhaging of talent from our own demographic which was the catalyst that called us to action. We joined forces to investigate whether better flexible working opportunities might be a way to address this and Flexible Teacher Talent was formed. Working with individuals and schools to improve flexible working in education, we soon saw that far from being 'just for mums', flexible working had the potential to benefit everyone.

Why are we fostering a flexible future in education?

- Improve pupil outcomes: We want to save schools money without sacrificing the quality of curriculum or teaching.
- Simplify working life: We want to prevent schools from being such a workplace lottery.

Why this book?

The biggest factor affecting whether a school accepts flexible practices is the viewpoint of view of the headteacher (DfE, 2019). Without them, there is no creation of a culture which promotes flexitime or late starts for teachers. Granting and encouraging flexible working requests or flexible job design does not happen. Meetings, parents' evenings, open evenings, performances, information events – there is so much that happens after school, even apart from just the workload of marking and planning. Balancing the needs of your life with the demands of your job is not easy for teachers and school leaders. A growing issue with workload has been exacerbated further due to a combination of funding cuts and increased accountability measures. It is difficult to find advertised part time roles as a classroom teacher and near impossible if you are a senior leader. Negotiating flexibility in post or when returning from maternity leave or another absence is by no means guaranteed and often difficult, loaded or frankly impossible.

Our expertise comes from making flexible working in the education sector our focus, from seeing it from many differing perspectives, which has helped us to build up a bank of specialist knowledge. We cannot claim to have spent the Malcolm Gladwell 10,000 hours on it yet, but what began as a 'hobby' of sorts has led to us spending more and more time reading, researching and discussing flexible work in education than any leader will have time to do. We want to share that knowledge and expertise as widely as possible; distil the benefits; offer practical, proven advice and share solutions and examples. Getting time with headteachers is notoriously difficult and they are the key factor in whether a school adopts flexible working or not.

We hope that this book will act as a practical guide for school leaders on introducing or improving flexible working in their schools. Those who are already working flexibly or aspiring to can learn from it and use it in their requests or practice. The more that schools see successful flexible working, the more widespread the practice will become, so there is a role to play for individuals working flexibly and for school leaders in improving the landscape. It is a chicken and egg scenario. Without schools offering and supporting flexible working there will be no successful examples of flexible working in the education sector, but those working flexibly also have a key role in shaping the narrative on flexibility for everyone. As flexible workers ourselves, we appreciate the strength and confidence it can take to challenge the status quo and explain and justify your position. We are conscious of how difficult that can be for individuals in a school or system that does not embrace flexibility, but each time someone fights for their flex, they make it easier for the next person in that position and over time we will see real change.

We are both potential statistics of teachers 'lost' due to lack of flexibility. We are both experienced, effective teachers and leaders who had worked confidently and successfully in education for more than a combined 20 years before having children. After the birth of our first children, we sought to work more flexibly but were not able to achieve our objectives. We recognise our significant privilege as white women in traditional family structures and even the most cursory consideration of intersectionality makes it safe to assume that if we were frustrated with the lack of flexible opportunities in the education system, then others with protected characteristics will have faced tougher barriers and for longer. Our aim is to remove these barriers for everyone and help avoid the 'workplace lottery'.

Much of the education sector is stuck in the dark ages when it comes to flexible working. There are many benefits that are missed if schools don't embrace it. Many teachers leave or choose not to return to teaching because they cannot access part time or other flexible working opportunities. Among secondary school teachers who leave the profession, the proportion working part-time increases by 20 percentage points when taking up a new job (DfE, 2019).

Besides part-time working, there is demand for other types of flexible working, including the opportunity to leave the school site if not teaching. Implemented successfully, flexible working should attract more people to join teaching, keep more people in teaching and encourage more to return.

We use case studies throughout the book to illustrate theoretical points in practice or give examples of best practice or different ways that flexibility can work. This first one is a personal story to highlight the importance of a school's approach to flexible working as part of wider school culture.

Case study 1.1 Lucy Rose

I returned to my Assistant Head role after maternity leave with my first child. In that school, the pervasive culture of presenteeism created a constant battle. It was hard to rectify the evidence of your successful work with endless references to your absence, 'days off', awkwardness about you not being there, 'difficulty' of having Senior Leaders (SLT) who were not always present. This at a time when I was most vulnerable. Like most new parents, I was sleep deprived and I had gone through a cataclysmic change in my life. After nine months away, I returned to school with less reintegration than if I had been off sick for more than three days. After any leave of absence, it is usual to have a meeting with a line manager. At the time, a wonderful, compassionate man had been left acting as head-teacher in complicated circumstances. He met with me and explained honestly that the incoming Multi-academy Trust would not agree to SLT working anything other than full time and the best thing he could do would be to suggest a starting point of three days a week so that I had leverage to negotiate to the inevitable four. The MAT did agree to four days but only for one year making it clear that 'next year we'll expect you in every day of the week, OK?'. It did not feel 'OK', it felt like I was being pushed beyond my capacity and that I was on a one-year-long probation.

The first meeting I attended was a whole staff briefing with the new academy chain discussing how the takeover would affect staff numbers, salaries and everyday life. I saw that my SLT were already under huge pressure, swamped with work to protect the school they had worked so hard in and, in spite of my needs, I did not feel this was the time to air them. Having no one with the apparent emotional capacity to discuss it with, I decided to simply return with 'no fuss' and help get the school back to where we knew it could be. That would be the best thing for everyone, wouldn't it? Asking for meaningful catch up on CPD I had missed, on any new school systems which had been implemented, a room to express milk in, who would be in charge of my responsibilities on my day off all seemed minimal, superfluous 'fuss' and I avoided talking about them, deciding just to make do.

It is easy to see what I would do differently now. I recognise that impostor syndrome is a reality which can be checked and balanced if discussed and shared with a support network or coach. The wonderful inception by Emma Sheppard of The MTPT Project means that a supportive nationwide network now exists for parent-teachers. Looking back, it seems pitiful and so simple to see how easily it could have been avoided. However, it has taken a long time to get to this point. My confident, outgoing pre-child self would never have recognised the person I became. I had never been an introvert or unable to speak up for myself or others and yet in this situation I felt silenced. It made me reflect how poorly other colleagues had been treated, often at times when they were most vulnerable and needed most care. Colleagues whose parents had died. Colleagues going through a relationship break-up. Colleagues who were exhausted and had no idea how to prioritise their own self-care and were labelled as having 'lost it'. Colleagues who had been brought in to reflect the student body and to increase diversity without making the environment safe for them. Instead of empathy, collaboration and support, energy was put into

(Continued)

evidence gathering, capability procedures and dismissal. This did not happen once or twice; it happened a lot. Yet there was no room given for reflection that the behaviour and attitude of the outgoing headteacher was responsible until it became obvious that the new failing Ofsted grading and subsequent takeover of the school was as a result of the lack of effective leadership.

We are not suggesting for a moment that everyone has the same experience as us. In fact, we are thrilled to have collected a wealth of stories where people have negotiated flexible working, had interviews and received promotions while navigating new parenthood. No one experience leaving for and returning from maternity leave is the same. Many people would have had a less toxic school culture to begin with and/or the confidence, resources and capacity to behave differently from the way we did. However, Lucy's story serves to highlight the workplace 'lottery' that many teachers only realise we have found ourselves in too late and when we are at our most vulnerable.

Characteristics of workplaces not conducive to flexible working include but are not limited to:

- Lack of investment in genuine staff wellbeing and an expectation that they will do 'whatever it takes' for the pupils in the school regardless of time
- Trope of the 'martyr' teachers who mistakenly prioritise their own wellbeing below the needs of their pupils
- 'Earned our stripes' culture of working long hours in challenging schools
- Expectation of presenteeism to demonstrate commitment
- Presenteeism outperforming demonstrative success of any other kind
- Lack of effective systems of communication when things are not perfect
- Lack of informed or effective HR staff or SLT with any HR experience to discuss legal workplace rights with staff returning from maternity leave
- Lack of robust two-way communication
- 'Toxic' or lack of transparency at leadership level
- Overworked and exhausted SLT who do not model work/life balance and do not have capacity to accommodate any new needs from staff
- Lack of empathy or capacity for staff who are not 'performing' for whatever reason
- Frequent examples of 'burn-out' because of the unrealistic and ineffective expectations of workload

You might recognise some of these characteristics and have experienced the negative impact they have on your teaching and interactions with young people. In Chapter 3, we look at examples of groups of people who might benefit from flexible working, but it is important that the existence of a genuinely flexible working culture serves to eradicate these negative tropes for everyone. If a school embraces flexible working, it must have effective HR and communication. If a school embraces flexibility, it cannot also have an unhealthy culture of presenteeism and long hours. If a school embraces flexibility, it cannot have leaders who do not look after their own wellbeing as a priority. Flexibility might be utilised more by certain groups of people but its existence benefits everyone.

How to use this book

In this book, we hope to provide evidence and practical examples of how flexible working can work in schools with the aim of making schools better places to work and therefore providing students with a better experience. We have written it as a guide for headteachers and school leaders, not just to convince you of the benefits but to give you pragmatic and useful ways to make the changes. If you are an individual teacher or school leader looking to work more flexibly, we hope that you can use the information and examples in this book to help you make your business case to your school for flexible working requests.

Reading routes

If you are already convinced about the benefits of flexible working in schools:

- go straight to Chapter 4. Chapters 4–6 are more practical and go into more specific detail about how flexible working can work in schools and more detailed advice on how it can be implemented and create particular benefits in different scenarios.

If you are a headteacher who is sceptical:

- read from Chapter 1 and engage with us on Twitter if you have any questions. Chapters 1–3 are more theoretical but include case studies of how schools and individuals work flexibly in schools.

If you are a teacher or leader looking to work flexibly in an organisation where you would be in the minority:

- read Chapters 1–3 and be mindful of the benefits of flexible working to reassure yourself that you are doing the right thing and convince others if needed.

If you are a teacher or leader looking to make a flexible working request:

- read Chapters 4–6 with a view to applying them to your own school context to form a business case in a flexible working request, plus Chapters 7 or 8 depending on whether you would to prefer to work part-time or job-share.

If you are a leader who has stakeholders to convince:

- look at Chapters 2 and 3 for the benefits and Chapters 4–6 for addressing more practical concerns.

If you are a school leader who is ready to go 'full flex':

- read Chapters 7–9 for more detailed case studies about different ways to offer flexibility and develop those working flexibly in your school.

Summary

This chapter has described:

- Who we are and why we wrote this book
- Why we feel this book is important and needed
- How you might use this book, depending on what you are hoping to get out of it

References

Department for Education (2019) *Teacher Recruitment and Retention Strategy*. London: Department for Education.

Department for Education (2014) *School Workforce in England Data*. London: Department for Education.

Policy Exchange (2016) *The Importance of Teachers*. London. Policy Exchange.

Sharp, C., Smith, R., Worth, J. and Van den Brande, J. (2019) *Part-Time Teaching and Flexible Working in Secondary Schools*. Slough: NFER

2

THE BENEFITS OF FLEXIBLE WORKING IN EDUCATION

In this chapter we will:

- Look at general benefits of flexible working for organisations and individuals
- Apply these benefits to the education sector by looking at how they relate to teachers and schools
- Consider positive impacts for productivity, recruitment, retention, diversity, staff wellbeing, cost savings and future generations.

Introduction

The benefits of flexible working in general have been well documented for many years in the commercial world, such as increased productivity, benefits for recruitment and retention and increased workforce diversity (Cannon and Elford, 2017). The Agile Future Forum (Cannon, 2019) showed that existing agile working practices in UK businesses were yielding value equivalent to between 3 and 13 per cent of total workforce costs and that more extensive or innovative flexible working could save up to a further 7 per cent and boost sales by up to 11 per cent. They cite increased productivity, increased quality of output, attraction and retention of a high-quality talent pool and minimising costs as key factors in this. Not only are these benefits applicable in the education sector, they are vitally important.

Increased productivity in schools means better outcomes for pupils – no one can disagree with the importance of that. It also means better value for money in terms of public spending – at a time when the fiscal pressures on governments across the world are mounting, this is particularly important. Our sector is facing a dual threat of recruitment and retention issues alongside rising pupil numbers, a problem expected to worsen in coming years.

Flexible Teacher Talent was born because after researching the retention of women aged 30–39 in teaching, we believed that better flexible working would begin to address this issue. We saw it as an opportunity to help retain some of the 6,000 women aged 30–39 who are leaving the profession each year (Simons et al., 2016). We also saw the value in improving leadership opportunities for women so that the numbers in headship mirror the number in the profession (a particular problem in secondary schools). We saw how flexible working could retain a body of teachers and leaders who were both parents and teachers.

Building on our initial research led us to see that the benefits of flexible working in our schools were far wider reaching. Consider who requests flexibility most frequently; women aged 30–39, but also parents of all ages and genders, those with caring responsibilities for elderly or ill parents or other family members and teachers and leaders nearing retirement. In essence, those demanding flexible working are often the most experienced, effective teachers and leaders in our schools. Retaining them has a direct impact on pupil outcomes, but also benefits the wider school community. Research from the Sutton Trust (2011) shows that over a school year, pupils from disadvantaged backgrounds gain 1.5 years' worth of learning with very effective teachers, compared with 0.5 years with poorly performing teachers. These experienced, effective teachers are also the mentors, coaches and role models who support and inspire new generations of teachers and leaders. Retaining them has benefits for succession planning and handovers when leaders retire or move on. They hold so much organisational knowledge and can pass it on to new recruits to ensure the smooth running of the school year.

In addition, we looked at who it would attract to the profession. Education is competing with so many other industries and professions who use flexible working as part of a suite of perks and as a means of attracting the best graduates to work at their firms. Some will say that teaching is a vocation and you sign up because you want to make a difference in the lives of the young people you work with, so why should we have to worry about attracting those considering other options or who are changing careers? The numbers show that we do not have enough teachers or leaders in the pipeline for our schools, so we need to find them from somewhere. If we are to make teaching sustainable, we must welcome colleagues in the profession who pursue other interests. As well as family commitments, retirement and their own health, staff may need flexibility for being involved in a charity, starting up a new business, writing a book, taking on a voluntary position or training for a sporting event. There is much to gain from retaining staff involved in their own personal growth or the wellbeing of the community outside of the school gate.

Looking beyond these benefits to individuals and organisations, there are obvious benefits for recruitment and retention and there is a need to catch up with and compete with other sectors who are already reaping the benefits of more flexible ways of working. The ultimate benefit of flexible working is that it can get and keep effective teachers and leaders in our schools which will have a direct and positive impact on pupil outcomes.

Recruitment

School leaders often face difficulties in recruiting teachers and leaders. A 2017 NAHT survey showed that 81 per cent of headteachers found it difficult to fill teaching vacancies, they struggled to recruit for 63 per cent of vacancies and failed to recruit in nearly a fifth of cases (18 per cent). Staffing the school is crucial to its smooth and effective operation and failing to appoint staff can have serious implications both financially and in terms of the quality of teaching and learning and leadership. In situations where class teachers cannot be appointed, schools often turn to high-cost supply agencies. As well as being relatively expensive (NEU, 2020 suggests nearly 10 per cent of supply teachers are paid more than £150 per day), there can also be difficulties with settling in, building relationships and quality of pedagogy. Where there are gaps in leadership positions, more responsibility and pressure is added to the workload of others. This leads to situations where senior leaders have to take on tasks that middle leaders or classroom teachers should be doing, or classroom teachers are left without guidance and resources. NAHT (2017) data show 44 per cent of schools need SLT to cover lessons. In a profession where workload is already seen as unmanageable, unfilled vacancies make the situation even worse. NFER research (Worth and Walker, 2019) reported that workload is a 'fairly' or 'very' serious problem in around seven out of ten primary and nine out of ten secondary schools. The research showed that 74 per cent of teachers, middle leaders and senior leaders reported not achieving a good work–life balance and 79 per cent reported not having an acceptable workload.

So how can flexible working help? Advertising posts with flexibility can actually increase the application conversion rate on applications by up to 19 per cent according to TES data (TESGlobalCorp, 2017). This increases the chances of being able to recruit successfully, which is beneficial particularly in secondary subjects where there is a real shortage of applicants. For Sciences, advertising flexibly can increase your chances of success by 13 per cent. Stating a commitment to flexibility, even for full-time posts, can make the role and school more attractive to potential candidates (more on recruitment in Chapter 6).

It is not just young or new teachers who want flexibility. NowTeach is a training and development scheme for career changers who want to become teachers. Their programme is four days a week rather than full time, and the majority of their trainees work flexibly once trained. There are around 260,000 qualified teachers not working in state schools in England (Worth, 2020), 87,000 of them are under age 40; maybe a better offer in terms of flexible working could entice them back? This is of crucial importance given teacher shortages. DfE census data (Department for Education, 2020) on teacher recruitment and retention show the labour market for secondary teachers continues to face a significant and increasing challenge, made worse by increasing pupil numbers, which are set to continue growing by a further 11 per cent in the five years until 2023/2024 (Worth, 2020). The national picture for teacher supply in primary schools is more stable with recruitment and retention figures looking stronger but there continue to be challenges at a local level and in terms of filling school leadership posts.

Case study 2.1 John Taylor Free School, Burton-on-Trent

In the process of setting up the new John Taylor Free School in Staffordshire, Sue Plant was 'determined that flexibility will be at the heart of what we're doing'. John Taylor is a secondary comprehensive school which opened in September 2018 with Year 7 and will have around 1,550 11- to 18-year-old students (including 350 at Post-16) when it reaches capacity. Sue believes that teaching should be compatible with having a family and the pursuit of other interests. She is hugely passionate about flexibility in education and believes that allowing teachers to work flexibly adds value to them as individuals as well as to their impact on pupils. In a local area where other headteachers are struggling to recruit, the new school was fully staffed, on budget and ready for its opening in 2018 having spent £0 on recruitment.

The offer of flexibility was well received. The initial meeting about the new school claimed that 'flexibility is important to us' and the open meeting attracted 400 attendees. Four hundred! Specific roles were not advertised but she shared the subjects needed and then titles were created once Sue had met and interviewed the candidates. There was a wide field of candidates to choose from with 160 applicants for those initial 11 jobs, including 15 for maths and 6 for music. There was little resistance from the Multi-academy Trust or the governors: if you are attracting high quality people with the right values, who can argue with getting the right people on the team?

The design and technology teacher works 0.8 so that he can do his own design work in his studio one day a week. The music teacher was attracted by the ethos of the school and also works 0.8 to practise his considerable musical talents. For another member of staff who has a young family, a leadership level post was agreed and she began her first year at the school working 0.6. Transparency and clear communication from the start means that the flexible policy works for everyone. As Sue explains, 'The existence of MATs means that leadership no longer has to follow a linear structure and there are possibilities which did not exist five years ago' and that 'While there is a certain freedom in setting a school up from scratch, we must encourage people in existing schools to be more creative about possibilities'.

As the school has grown, the flexibility in recruitment has continued. Sue still spends very little on recruitment, hosting recruitment open days and using social media rather than paying for expensive adverts. The reputation of the school's flexible approach and strong leadership means that positive word of mouth results in any roles available having a great deal of interest. In fact, Sue has spoken about a number of applicants relocating specifically to work flexibly at John Taylor Free School. In a competitive job market for teachers, she is attracting talent from across the country.

Retention

Recruitment and retention are obviously linked: if you can keep your teachers and leaders, you will have fewer new staff to recruit. Keeping your staff happy and well developed should be a high priority in any case because happy staff are more productive and that means better outcomes for pupils. But good retention and low staff turnover have other benefits. It saves money and time on recruitment, and it is also about who you have in the classroom and staffroom, not simply filling the vacancies. Keeping experienced and effective staff who have built an understanding of not only the school systems but also of the children themselves has many benefits for a school. They are the people who train, coach and mentor new teachers, who understand how the school works and who drive changes and progress. Keeping hold of them saves money on recruitment and training, but its value is so much more in terms of the experience for children in their classroom and the teachers in their teams.

NAHT data (2017) shows two-thirds (66 per cent) of school leaders said they were aware that some of their staff left the teaching profession for reasons other than retirement. The top two reasons cited were workload (84 per cent of respondents) and work–life balance (83 per cent of respondents). Women aged 30–39 are one of the biggest groups leaving teaching. Figures from the Department for Education's Database of Teacher Records (2016) show about 6,000 (27 per cent) of teachers who left the profession in 2013 were women aged between 30 and 39. This demographic represents about 23 per cent of the profession, but we do not expect qualified teachers to leave so long before retirement age, although it is not hard to guess why they might be leaving. This is the age when many people choose to start a family and for some (too many) people, teaching and school leadership are not seen as compatible with parenting. A study by The MTPT Project (Sheppard, 2020) has shown the importance for this demographic of flexible working practices. The lack of opportunity to work flexibly in schools is a key factor in the decision of many teachers and leaders to leave the profession. If even some of these leaving teachers could be retained by offering flexible working, then the benefits would be realised.

At a leadership level, these women do not become any less effective, talented or experienced because they want to work flexibly. One of the contributing factors to the gender pay gap in the education sector, which is one of the worst median gender pay gaps in the United Kingdom at 19.7 per cent (Guibourg, 2018), is the relatively poor offer of flexibility in schools. It has been common for many years to see flexible working requests from middle and senior leaders turned down because the role cannot be done flexibly. Surely our experience during the COVID-19 situation has taught us that schools can be led remotely and flexibly, so certainly departments and key stages, line management areas and classes can be too. Childcare and other caring responsibilities still predominantly fall to women in our society, and over 75 per cent of teachers are women. If those women feel they have to choose between family responsibilities and work, then we end up with a situation where people are either forced out of the profession or continue to work while struggling to balance other responsibilities.

There is evidence that it is not just those with parenting or caring responsibilities whom schools would retain if they offered greater flexible working opportunities. A Chartered Institute of Personnel and Development (CIPD) study in 2016 showed that 76 per cent of employers improved their retention of staff after introducing flexible working.

Wellbeing

In the foreword of Kat Howard's book *Stop Talking About Wellbeing*, Mary Myatt talks about the 'wellbeing agenda' and the need to restore balance and boundaries. Beside the moral obligation to treat teachers and school leaders as humans and recognise their needs, desires, preferences and mental and physical health, looking after the wellbeing of your staff is important for other reasons. Many businesses understand that their people are their greatest resource: if they look after their employees, their customers' needs will be better met and their enterprise will thrive. In terms of schools, this means so much: a better experience for pupils; retention of happy, productive staff; higher productivity which means better student outcomes and value for money from public spending. Flexible working is not the silver bullet for teacher wellbeing or addressing workload concerns. In fact, we state categorically that unmanageable workload is not a good reason for working flexibly. Not being able to do your job in the hours you are paid for is a workload management issue and the responsibility of school leaders to address.

However, flexible working is very much linked to wellbeing. Being able to work flexibly can allow teachers and school leaders to balance and blend their work life and their personal commitments, passions and aspirations. There are many reasons why allowing people to work flexibly can improve their wellbeing. It may allow them the time and space to spend time with their families, care for elderly or unwell parents, start a business, write a book, pursue a hobby or have more leisure time. A school where all staff are full-time and work long hours with no flexibility will often find their staff have a limited 'shelf life'. Staff work flat out for a few years then burnout or they leave because they do not see work as compatible with starting a family or pursuing another interest. It is not sustainable and the loss of experience and costs of recruitment and re-training often outweigh the benefits of having those staff without commitments who can work extremely long hours for a short period of time. Workplaces full of workaholics without perspective can quickly become toxic and not appealing or enjoyable places to work. It is important to model and promote a healthy working environment and flexible working is one way to do this.

Schools that are flexible-friendly also tend to be 'life-friendly', and genuinely value the wellbeing of their staff. Improved communication, accountability, trust and engagement are features of schools with a healthy flexible working culture. Whatever the reason people have chosen to work flexibly, being able to do so allows them to have a much better experience of work life balance. The chances of burnout and overstretching that affects and hampers so many in the teaching profession are lessened not just because people are able to work flexibly but because of the cultures in the schools that encourage them to do so. Consider the alternative to granting flexible working requests: staff leave, or they stay and work inflexibly. This might mean working full-time when they do not want to, missing school drop-off and pick-up for their own children, fitting nursing home or hospital visits or appointments in around the school day. Consider the potential impact on the motivation, commitment, health and attendance of these teachers and leaders. Allowing staff to work flexibly helps school to benefit from the best of these people. You can reap the rewards of their motivation, their commitment and their productivity. Those allowed to work flexibly often miss less work time. They make appointments and attend personal meetings or events outside of their working week. They often miss fewer workdays due to illness or other incidents.

At the heart of the link between flexible working and wellbeing is the fact that teachers and leaders are human. Requests for flexible working often come when people are at the most vulnerable or challenging time of their lives. Maybe they have just become a parent for the first time, a partner or parent required care or they are unwell or recovering. It may also be that they are requesting flexibility because they want to pursue a passion or an enterprise or maybe they have just come to a realisation about how they want to live their life.

Flexibility is by no means the only factor contributing to wellbeing and it should be used in conjunction with empathy, communication and a sensible and effective approach to workload and accountability. Imagine the impact on wellbeing of individuals where a flexible working request which is turned down or one that is granted but poorly managed. Equally, imagine the benefits for wellbeing of having open and positive conversations with all staff about how they want their working week to look. Something which may make a significant positive impact on a teacher's wellbeing might be easy for a school to accommodate, yet unless schools are open to the idea of flexible working this will not happen.

If we do not ensure, first and foremost, that our teachers are feeling physically and mentally well, they cannot be their best for their students. Consequently, a school which does not prioritise staff wellbeing is disadvantaging its own students.

(Tomsett and Uttley, 2020)

Productivity

When it comes to flexible working, education is about 30 years behind other sectors. According to a 2017 study of 20,000 businesses, 72 per cent reported that flexible working increased productivity (Regus, 2017). Perpetual Guardian, a finance company in New Zealand, working with The University of Auckland and Auckland University of Technology (AUT), claimed productivity has increased by up to 20 per cent after reducing all employees to a four day working week (4 Day Week, 2019). Some big names have announced huge changes in flexibility in recent years all PriceWaterhouseCooper staff can now work flexibly (BBC, 2018), and this is set to continue as businesses see the cost benefit of forced remote working during COVID-19 and move to hybrid working models. In education, an increase in 'productivity' is an improvement in pupil outcomes. We cannot, therefore, afford to miss out on the potential benefits that flexible working could bring to both our pupils and our staff.

We know that happier staff are more productive and that those working flexibly are more productive and happier, so flexible working increases productivity from a number of different angles. According to a Cranfield University research report (Kelliher, 2008) on flexible workers, 97 per cent of managers said the quantity of their work improved or stayed the same and 93 per cent said the quality of the work improved or stayed the same. It is highly likely that achieving the same or more while working flexibly will lead to increased job satisfaction which has a further positive impact on wellbeing, commitment and productivity. According to research by the International Workplace Group (IWG, 2019) in the United States, 85 per cent of businesses say that offering more flexibility has increased productivity.

Flexible working can reduce workload in the case of part-time or job-sharing but it can also allow workload to be managed more effectively for full-time staff making them more productive. If people are allowed to choose when, how and where they work during non-contact time, then they are likely to be more engaged and productive. If school leaders can complete strategic or managerial tasks from home rather than in school with constant interruptions, distractions and firefighting, they are likely to be more efficient.

Working flexibly or part-time can allow greater focus for people when they do set aside time to work. Working remotely can have benefits too. It reduces commuting time, allows people to work at a time and in an environment that they find productive and is good for their wellbeing. It allows them to work at times when they cannot go into school, but can work. For example, if you have to attend an appointment or be at home with a poorly child, you cannot go in to work but you can work remotely or from home. Equally, as many of us have now experienced, if you are infectious or potentially infectious but asymptomatic or feeling well then working remotely allows you to work without increasing risk for others.

> *Part time staff are an untapped resource in many schools; but with the right support, they can be the strongest members of any departmental team as the balance that they seek is fulfilled – and as a result, they can sometimes be the most productive, most positive forces within a department, and incredibly supportive of full-time staff where the challenges are different.*
>
> (Howard, 2020)

Savings

We have already mentioned savings in terms of recruitment costs if staff are retained, but there are other reasons why flexible working makes good financial sense.

In secondary schools, you can increase efficiency and save money through lean timetabling, when you only employ teachers for as many hours as you need them. If you need an extra A Level maths teacher for an additional class, you don't need to hire a full-time maths teacher who then spends 15 hours a week teaching computing or economics as a non-specialist. Part-time teachers can allow better specialisation as well as reducing the numbers of staff who are under hours on their teaching load. Part-time staff may be willing to adjust their hours each year depending on pupil numbers. For example, if there are fewer Year 10 students on a particular GCSE course, it may be possible to change a contract to 0.6 from 0.8 timetable to balance teaching loads with hours required. Given the nature of option choices and changing cohorts, this can be a cost-efficient solution.

At both primary and secondary levels, flexibility can be used at a leadership level to save money. Senior and middle leaders are paid at higher rates, so if their roles can be slimmed down while maintaining effectiveness, then the savings can be significant. Condensing their role so that they can do it across four days a week saves 20 per cent of their wage cost. Evidence also points to further areas of financial advantage. Reduced staff absence rates mean fewer supply teachers required, which reduces the bill for cover.

In less tangible terms, it is also common for part-time teachers to give much more than their pro rata in terms of work. While there are moral, and legal, issues with asking or expecting employees to work more than they are paid for, it is often the case that part-time teachers do more than the proportion of the work they are contracted to do.

These favourable financial implications must of course be offset against additional costs such as a rise in oncosts due to increased head count and considering extra hours for job-share handovers and so on. But the balance of financial gain and burden seems very much to support the argument for flexible working.

Case study 2.2 Furzedown Primary School, Wandsworth

Initially to decrease staff salaries in the wake of budget cuts, Furzedown Primary asked their staff which hours they would ideally work. The staff consultation began in 2017–2018 and since then, flexible working has evolved to suit the needs of the staff. The headteacher Monica Kitchlew-Wilson made the offer and left it open to staff to consider. As a result of the consultation, the school has three experienced members of SLT on 4 or 4.5 days per week which created a salary saving of around £60k.

Monica recognised loyalty from younger teachers offering to work fewer days to reduce the school's costs but did not accept that they should take a cut in salary just to improve the financial situation of the school. She understood that they would be moving towards applying for mortgages in order to remain (and teach) in the local area so she turned down their offers to help the school unless it was coming from their genuine desire to work more flexibly rather than just saving the school money.

Furzedown Primary does not have recruitment and retention problems; they have very low staff turnover, but taking the opportunity to find out what staff wanted in terms of flexibility has had a really positive effect for work/life balance. Prior to this, there would be regular requests for unpaid leave for cheaper flight tickets or music events during term time. Flexibility avoids the need for that and everyone is happier.

Each year group has three teachers for two classes of children. As the two classes are not always split in the same way, the attitude of the children is that 'these teachers teach my class' rather than, 'this is my class teacher'. Every teacher in the year group can be flexible and not everyone has to work full time. In one year group, for example, there is one teacher on a 0.9 contract, one on 0.8 and one on 0.6. The school never pays out for supply and is only paying the salary of 2.3 people. The children are used to different people teaching them; they know the teachers really well and the teachers plan together offering the experience and creativity of 'three brains'. Monica suggests that headteachers should: 'Move away from the supply teacher model to working with your staff for benefit of the children; it is a much healthier way to staff your school'.

Diversity

The findings of the 2018 McKinsey 'Diversity Matters' report are well documented. Without offering flexibility, there is a risk that schools end up with homogenous types of people in teacher and school leader roles. If the only people who can work in a school are those who can work full-time, start early, finish late and who do not have any commitments or interests that interfere with their work life, then you will end up with a very narrow talent pool and a limited set of views. Opening up roles at all levels to those wishing to work flexibly, allows school to retain and bring in staff with a range of experiences and social skills. It prevents the exclusion of parents, career changers, those with other caring responsibilities, those wishing to have portfolio careers or pursue other interests. Thinking about the diversity of views and depth and breadth of understanding and ideas they can bring shows how important it is to support them in working flexibly. Schools that are open to flexible working tend to have considered the work–life balance for all members of staff, which prevents burnout and helps all staff thrive.

Role models for the world of work

Lack of flexibility in the workplace creates unhealthy life modelling for the next generation. If children in our schools see women leaving after becoming parents, if they see men progressing quicker than women, if they see single parents stuck at a certain progression point, if they don't see anyone working part-time with responsibility – what messages does this send to them about work, parenting, gender roles and equality in the workplace? In a profession dominated by women, what is the messaging if the majority of CEOs, headteachers and SLT are male? In a profession where research since the 1970s indicates that a staff body should reflect the students they serve, what is the messaging if those at the top are white and male? Schools are the first organisations that most children have experience and understanding of. The way these organisations are set up and how they look after and develop their people will impact on how they understand organisational behaviour as they grow up. Normalising flexible working in schools is important if we want to grow a generation of future workers and managers who are successful in their careers and lives. We do not want children to grow up thinking that if you have caring responsibilities or a passion you want to pursue, then you must give up your career. We do not want children to see reinforced stereotypes of women having no choice but to conform to full-time parenting roles and men to full-time work time and again because of the way our organisations work.

Summary

This chapter has described:

- How the benefits of flexible working apply to teachers and schools
- Why the positive impact goes beyond individuals to benefit schools and ultimately pupils
- Practical and more philosophical benefits of flexible working in schools

References

4 Day Week (2019). White Paper: The Four-Day Week. Available at: https://4dayweek.com/four-day-week-trial/ (accessed July 2020).

BBC (2018). Work when you want, firm tells new staff. *BBC News*. Available at: https://www.bbc.co.uk/news/business-45353786

Cannon, F. (2019). *Agility Mindset: How Reframing Flexible Working Delivers Competitive Advantage*. London: Palgrave Macmillan.

Cannon, F. and Elford, N. (2017). *The Agility Mindset: How Reframing Flexible Working Delivers Competitive Advantage*. Cham, Switzerland: Palgrave Macmillan.

CIPD (April, 2016). *Employee Outlook Focus on Commuting and Flexible Working*. London: CIPD. Available at: https://www.cipd.co.uk/Images/employee-outlook-focus-on-commuting-and-flexible-working_tcm18-10886.pdf

Cranfield University (2018). *Flexible Working and Performance*. Bedfordshire: Cranfield University.

Department for Education (2020, 25 June) *School Workforce in England*. London: Department for Education. Available at: https://explore-education-statistics.service.gov.uk/find-statistics/school-workforce-in-england

Guibourg, C. (2018). Gender pay gap: Six things we've learnt. *BBC News*. Available at: https://www.bbc.co.uk/news/business-43668187 (accessed 7 April).

Howard, K. (2020). *Stop Talking About Wellbeing*. Melton: John Catt.

IWG (2019). *New Research Shows That Flexible Working is Now a Top Consideration in the War for Talent*. Luxembourg: IWG. www.prnewswire.com. Available at: https://www.prnewswire.com/news-releases/new-research-shows-that-flexible-working-is-now-a-top-consideration-in-the-war-for-talent-300818790.html

Kelliher, C. (2008). *Flexible Working and Performance*. Bedfordshire: Cranfield University/Working Families.

NAHT (2017). *The Leaky Pipeline Recruitment And Retention 2017 #TheLeakyPipeline*. Haywards Heath: NAHT. Available at: https://www.naht.org.uk/_resources/assets/attachment/full/0/92385.pdf

NEU (2020). *Supply Teachers – Pay, Conditions and Working Time*. London: NEU. Available at: https://neu.org.uk/advice/supply-teachers-pay-conditions-and-working-time (accessed 7 August 2020).

Regus (2017). *The Workplace Revolution: A Picture of Flexible Working 2017*. Available at: https://www.regus.com/work-us/wp-content/uploads/sites/131/2017/06/GBS-Report.pdf

Sheppard, E. (2020) MTPT Research. Available at: https://www.mtpt.org.uk/research/ (accessed July 2020).

Simons, J., Berry, D., Gertler, C., Jones, G., Lee, E., Metcalf, C., Rao, K. and Roberts, A. (2016). The Importance of Teachers A Collection of Essays on Teacher Recruitment and Retention. Available at: https://policyexchange.org.uk/wp-content/uploads/2016/09/the-Importance-of-Teachers.pdf (accessed 7 August 2020).

Sutton Trust (September, 2011) *Improving the Impact of Teachers on Pupil Achievement in the UK – Interim Findings*. London: Sutton Trust. Available at: https://www.suttontrust.com/our-research/improving-impact-teachers-pupil-achievement-uk-interim-findings/ (accessed 7 August 2020).

TESGlobalCorp (2017). *Flexible Working Recruitment Insights*. London: TES. Available at: https://www.slideshare.net/TESGlobalCorp/flexible-working-recruitment-insights (accessed 7 August 2020).

Tomsett, J. and Uttley, J. (April, 2020) *Putting Staff First: A Blueprint for Revitalising Our Schools*. Melton: John Catt.

Worth, J. and Walker, M. (2019, 25 October). *The Latest Findings From the Teacher Workload Survey 2019*. Slough: NFER. Available at: https://www.nfer.ac.uk/news-events/nfer-blogs/the-latest-findings-from-the-teacher-workload-survey-2019/ (accessed 21 December 2019).

Worth, J. (2020). *Teacher Labour Market in England: Annual Report 2020*. Slough: NFER. Available at: https://www.nfer.ac.uk/media/4063/tlm_annual_report_2020.pdf

3

REASONS FOR SEEKING FLEXIBLE WORKING IN SCHOOLS

In this chapter, we will:

- Consider the range of reasons why people may seek to work flexibly in education
- Explore in more depth the reasons why teachers may wish to work flexibly
- Outline the benefits from accommodating flexible working for these different groups

Introduction

In this chapter, we will examine in more detail who may want flexibility and why. There are a whole host of reasons why teachers may wish to work flexibly. Not everyone will want to work flexibly, but many will need or desire flexibility at some point in their career. We advocate that schools offer flexibility to everyone and that senior leaders evaluate individual circumstances annually with the aim of making it work wherever possible. Making flexibility part of the culture and 'the way we do things' allows for teaching to be a sustainable, lifelong career. However, for school leaders who are cautious or yet to be convinced by this approach, a good place to start may be looking at various reasons why teachers may request flexible working and explore how offering it to these groups may benefit a school.

This chapter is at risk of being a selection of stories about vulnerable people and 'worst-case' scenarios when schools need to adopt flexibility unless you accept that, at some point, for whatever reason, *you* might not choose to work a full week throughout the school year. If flexibility is something which can only be sought when someone is at their most vulnerable, it is likely to be difficult and ineffective. However, if it is the proactive core of your HR strategy, it empowers staff to be the best they can be for their pupils, not in spite of but because of what else is happening in their lives.

While 'mums' make up the majority of those seeking flexible working in schools, there are countless other groups and individuals looking for flexibility in other sectors far ahead of education. There are many reasons why teachers and school leaders may wish to work flexibly and for each, allowing them flexibility can bring many and varied benefits for the individual, the school and, ultimately, the pupils they serve. Encouraging flexible working for everyone can begin to address the gender pay gap in education and right the gender and race imbalance in school leadership. In terms of recruitment, it can allow us to attract graduates and career changers and keep them in teaching rather than losing them to other professions. If flexibility can be offered to teachers and leaders, it can retain their expertise and allow smoother and improved succession planning and transitions for new staff. Embracing flexible working allows schools to benefit from a richer tapestry of people who bring different skills, experiences and passions to schools.

Those with parenting and caring responsibilities

Childcare is the most common reason for flexible working requests from those in the education sector (Wooley, 2020). It is common for parents to want to work more flexibly to accommodate childcare responsibilities or spending more time with their children. It is a choice for each individual, for each family. There is no right and wrong; people should be able to choose whether they want to work full-time, part-time or not at all. There are obviously constraints to this; finances, health, circumstance. However, availability of flexible working opportunities should not be one of them.

> *There was strong consensus from HR professionals that employees sought flexible working arrangements to accommodate their caring responsibilities: primarily children, but also elderly parents. Childcare responsibilities mentioned included the school run, dealing with home emergencies, or transitioning back to work after parental leave.*
>
> (Nicks et al., 2019)

Childcare and other caring responsibilities such as looking after disabled, poorly or elderly family members often prevent people from working in traditional full-time roles and require flexibility if they are to continue or begin working. Timewise Foundation (2017) research identified a gender gap in the reasons for requesting flexibility, with 42 per cent of female part-time employees citing care responsibilities as a motivation for part-time working, compared to 17 per cent of male employees. Failing to offer flexible working has a negative impact on schools and on the gender pay gap in education. Women are more likely than men to apply for flexible working because they are more likely to be the ones with caring responsibilities for children or others. If the options are traditional, full-time posts or nothing, then women will be disproportionately affected by this. The Motherhood Penalty comes into play in an obvious way in a profession dominated by women. Remember, it was only 100 years ago that women had to give up teaching once they married.

> *The education sector has one of the worst gender pay gaps of all sectors in the UK with women receiving 80p for every £1 that men earn.*
>
> (Barr et al., 2019)

While men make up 24% of the education workforce, 33% of headteachers are male. Only the construction and finance industries have worse gender pay gap figures than education (DfE Workforce Data, 2019). In state-funded primary and nursery schools, only 14 per cent of all teachers are men and yet they make up 27 per cent of headteachers. In secondary schools, 36 per cent of teachers are men and yet 62 per cent of headteachers are male (DfE, 2019). Just read that again. In a profession dominated by women, most of the headteachers are men. The picture at CEO level of MATs is even worse. Needless to say (but we will, because they are already working twice as hard for half as much and it needs shouting about), as with all other sectors, the balance is even worse for our global majority ('BAME') colleagues. In state funded schools in England, 86.6 per cent of classroom teachers are White British or Irish, but they make up 94.7 per cent of headteachers. Asian women make up 4.4 per cent of the teaching workforce, but only 1.2 per cent of headteachers. Black teachers make up 2.3 per cent of the teaching workforce and 1 per cent of headteachers (DfE, 2019). With a role to play in education for setting the scene for future generations in terms of career aspirations and work/life blend, it is vital that we do better.

> *The education sector was again responsible for some of the largest discrepancies between male and female employees. Many of the companies with the biggest gaps favouring men were multi-academy trusts and independent schools according to Guardian analysis.*
>
> (Barr et al., 2019)

There is a perception that teaching and school leadership is a great career for women and mothers – long holidays, finishing at 3.30 pm, sector dominated by females. Anyone who works in schools knows this is not true: why is it seemingly so difficult to combine parenting with a career in teaching? Flexible Teacher Talent began to help address the haemorrhaging of talent from our schools. We met at the Teach First Innovation Unit where we had both submitted separate projects related to more agile, more dynamic, more flexible teaching. Lindsay was pushing for more availability of leadership positions which were not full time, and Lucy was looking to set up a kind of national dating agency where leaders could partner up and lead together. We came to it from an individual perspective, but through research realised we were in danger of being part of the 6,000 women aged 30–39 who leave the profession each year (Policy Exchange, 2016). Why do we see that peak of women leaving at the age when they are starting a family? However enlightened our times, however varied the look of individual families, women are still the main carers for young children and deal with the lion's (read lioness') share of not just the caring itself but also the mental load which goes with that. Not just the physical nursery pick up and drop off but remembering and packing all of the items which are required and listening to and acting upon all of the feedback given in the two-minute handover of your baby to an almost complete stranger (albeit a stranger you have chosen), for now, to take care of the most important thing in your life. Much of this could be mitigated against by having a more balanced allocation of roles, but the data demonstrates that it is not, yet. So, in the meantime, we need to accommodate that when designing job roles in our schools.

As well as the caring, the mental load and the emotional turmoil/freedom of those first drop offs, there are new logistical concerns. Who drops your child off at school/ nursery when you have to be in your own workplace before the start of the school day? What about once your children start school? Maybe a breakfast and after school club exists at their primary school, but what about that potentially difficult transition to secondary when they begin to take the bus alone? What if you are a single parent? Colleagues lucky enough to have children know that their children will always need them, and without flexible options at all levels, we are asking staff who are parents to decide between committing time to their own children and the children they teach. Spoiler alert: there is no choice.

More than half of teachers are also parents themselves (TeacherTapp, 2017). More than half of teachers who leave to look after children never return (NFER, 2015). Parents of children of all ages may benefit from more flexibility in their working patterns. They bring so much to our schools and to the mentoring of newer colleagues – can we really afford to lose them? Forcing teachers and school leaders to choose between work and caring responsibilities will impact more on women. Lack of diversity in leadership breeds further lack of diversity and empathy for those who need to work differently, so it is self-perpetuating.

Schools that are family friendly are also life friendly. Teachers are humans; treating them as such allows schools not only to retain them but also to get the best from them. Having a child or a sick or disabled relative or partner does not make people any less good at their jobs; they are not any less skilled or experienced, they just may not be able to work in the same way that they did before. If schools can make adjustments and offer flexibility, then they can continue to benefit from those skills, experiences and qualities rather than lose them.

> *Schools with family friendly cultures and policies, make it easier for their employees to more easily balance work and life; in order to fulfil their obligations.*
>
> (Hayley Dunn, 2017)

Improved flexible working opportunities for senior leaders in schools would help to address the disparity in leadership appointments and pay. Other sectors often see more flexibility the more senior you are, but in teaching, this is not seen to be the case: headteachers and other senior leaders must apparently be on site at all times. The COVID-19 situation led to many schools having to operate remotely with minimal numbers of staff and students on site, so maybe this will help to promote the idea that school leaders can work effectively from home. If men and women can work flexibly at all levels in schools, then it will not be seen as such a barrier to progression. Women will be better represented in senior roles and it will not be the case that those who want or need to work flexibly can only work as classroom teachers no matter what their previous level of experience or potential.

Case study 3.1 Emma Sheppard, Maternity Teacher Paternity Teacher Project

The Maternity Teacher Paternity Teacher (MTPT) Project began in 2016 when Emma started itching to do some continued professional development (CPD) while on maternity leave with her first child. It has grown from an effort to improve CPD opportunities for teachers on parental leave to a one stop shop for teachers before, during and after they become parents. They champion the rights of teachers and school leaders who also happen to be parents themselves and Emma fiercely advocates for any measures large or small which support parents in whatever level of development and progression they desire.

Research from The MTPT Project shows a clear link between leaving the profession or failure to progress when flexible working requests are rejected. 'When flexible working requests are agreed for middle and senior leaders, teacher progression continues. When requests are denied, teachers take a step back or lose their teaching and learning responsibility (TLR) as this is denied for those working part-time. In the worst-case scenario, they leave teaching altogether. After an initial 500 survey responses, we completed qualitative interviews with 38 respondents who had left the profession and 50% of those cited denial of flexible working as the principal reason for this'.

One of the many strands of support offered by The MTPT Project is advice on flexible working and many members are showing how progression, retention, return and success can be achieved as a parent in the teaching profession.

We do have success stories for schools that grant flexible working. Being able to offer them that flexibility in that very vulnerable period just after their maternity leave keeps them in school and in the profession.

Those with other interests

Teachers are interesting people. They are interested and curious and the great ones are lifelong learners. They have chosen a career where they will always be reflecting, improving and learning more. They are shaping the pupils in their care for a world which we cannot imagine and equipping them with skills for a future we cannot predict. It is fair to say that in our profession, we have people who are passionate about a whole range of stuff: real and imagined, which takes time to nurture, cultivate and share. Over the course of a lifetime, these interests will morph, develop and change from when our careers began. Lack of flexibility can seriously impede the enjoyment and fulfilment a teacher receives from a hobby which cannot always be ignored or forgotten during term time. Yes, there are holidays in which to pursue other interests, but suggesting that teachers leave part of what makes them interesting aside during term time is likely to lead to less happy and productive people with less joy and fewer interests to share with others.

Session musicians, marathon runners, graphic designers, food bank volunteers, flower arrangers, international bridge players, gardeners, open water swimmers, golfers, yogis and a wealth of other hobbies and expertise help make our teaching workforce and are just some of the reasons we know of that staff have used to request flexible working. On a flexible working request form, these interests might not seem as pressing or urgent as caring for a child or an elderly relative but they are important to the wellbeing of each individual.

Arguably, the art of marrying up hobbies and interests with a profession you love is an ideal which could be realised in advance of taking on often overwhelming caring responsibilities. A profession which values the whole person and allows them to pursue interests outside of teaching is investing in them as a long term, sustainable member of the workforce. Happier people are more productive and, in a profession where we are motivating and inspiring the young people in our care, serious recognition of the value of other interests is crucial to our success.

We advocate asking your staff whether they would take an element of flexibility, and what they would do with that time. What harm can it do to ask? You will be surprised at the results. People are complex and you will know each one of them better. A late start here and an early finish there will ensure that they find themselves bringing so much more energy and joy to a profession which they love and which is allowing them to be their whole selves.

It is wonderful to have teachers and school leaders who are passionate about pedagogy and educational research and theory. We should all be. In addition, there is also room and value in having a PE and health fanatic teaching A Level history, and a passionate historian teaching Key Stage 2. There is benefit from having school leaders who have developed empathy and coaching skills from experiences outside of education or who are able to think more strategically and with greater perspective because they spend some time each week doing something else that they love. Holly Power, Founder of Return to Teach, often talks about the value that part-time staff can bring to schools.

Case study 3.2 Holly Power, Return to Teach

Holly Power is CEO of Return to Teach, which is an organisation that matched teachers who could offer part-time or flexible hours with schools requiring specialist teachers. Holly created Return to Teach because as Assistant Principal responsible for Key Stage 5, she often found it difficult to recruit specialist teachers for A Level subjects. She also saw an important role for part-time teachers in terms of both their contribution to the school and in allowing lean, cost effective timetabling. Getting good teachers in front of the children who needed it the most and struggling to recruit at the same time as seeing effective teachers leave the profession was frustrating and motivated her to take action. Return to Teach saved the schools money on supply teachers (who in many cases were non-specialist or inexperienced in teaching in A Level), and allowed the Return to Teach candidates to teach only the number of hours a week they wished to.

Holly explains that, 'A lot of people want to do a Masters in Education, want to run their own business, do journalism, teach yoga – alongside a profession they love. To me, as a school leader, it has opened my eyes to the value flexible workers can bring to an organisation.'

What people do when not a teacher can add to their practice, it does not detract from it. A business teacher who also runs a business, an art teacher who also creates their own pieces, a primary school deputy who visits other schools every week, a class teacher studying to become an educational psychologist or a SENCO training to be an occupational therapist all add value to the school community.

Case study 3.3 Other interests

History

Dr Ed Shawcross, graduate of Oxford and UCL, who teaches History, used flexible working to reduce his timetable in order to spend time researching and writing academic books on nineteenth century Mexico and France. In addition to his class teaching, he leads an extended discussion group for A Level History students where they explore topics beyond the specification.

Wellbeing

Nic Owen worked three days a week as a primary school teacher while she researched health and fitness, spent time meditating and trained to be a wellbeing coach. The development of her own wellbeing business outside of the classroom helped her to understand and build self-esteem in the children she was working with in school.

Art

Nigel Murray has recently retired after a long career teaching Art. One of those teachers who made his mark on every student and colleague who worked with him, Nigel used

(Continued)

flexible working a number of times in his career. Most recently he was able to extend the time he spent working pre-retirement by working three shortened days a week. After spending months in 2015/2016 recovering from leukaemia, he returned to work flexibly. Working reduced hours in school has allowed him to work on his own art. He is currently a practising artist producing work for exhibitions and commissions (available at www.nigelmurrayart.co.uk).

Leadership

Amjad Ali is Assistant Head at a secondary school in Oxfordshire. He works four days a week in school on a 0.8 contract and then on Fridays he provides CPD for other schools and educators on topics such as behaviour and inclusion. His educational research and the time he spends in other schools and working with leaders across the country adds to the development of his own leadership practice. He is also co-founder of the @BAMEedNetwork promoting diversity across the education sector and working part-time gives him time to dedicate to this.

Those moving towards retirement

A study on working flexibly for gradual/partial retirement reported statistically significant improvements in health outcomes such as blood pressure and heart rate, tiredness, mental health, sleep duration, sleep quality, and alertness; as well as for secondary health outcomes such as social support and sense of community – no ill health effects were reported (Joyce et al., 2010).

How many of us know an experienced member of staff who provides CPD simply by modelling conversations with children, parents and staff which they have become experts in during their time in the profession? How many of us have known colleagues who are not thrown by the latest government guidelines or Ofsted frameworks because they have a deep-rooted knowledge of what works for the children and families in their care? How many of us know of schools which had a 'wobble' or a downgrade in inspection once a senior colleague left? There is a wealth of knowledge held by experienced teachers and leaders which it would be damaging for schools to lose due to lack of flexibility. In the right circumstances, retaining an experienced postholder might be exactly what is needed to help a new-to-the-post leader get off to a flying start.

Case study 3.4 St Peter's C.E. Primary School, Farnworth, Bolton

Lynn Williams began her career as a headteacher in a co-headship alongside the current, experienced headteacher who was planning to retire in the not too distant future. At the

(Continued)

time, she had a six-month-old baby, had completed her NQPH and was ready for headship. From 2006 to 2014, they worked three days a week each with one day of overlap and from September 2014, Lynn took over the substantive post. As Lynn rightly explains, 'most people would love to have that option of succession planning'.

Lynn is now the sole headteacher, but she is open to flexibility if it is outcome focused, 'teachers have to deliver exceptionally to the pupils...it does not matter which face you see as long as they deliver and that needs to be the focus'. The co-headship structure provided a strong, secure leadership base, combining leadership skills to ensure the highly challenging circumstances of the school did not detract the leaders from the core purpose of ensuring the maximum flourishing of all children. Whilst flexible, the co-headteachers also became inseparable, the voice of St. Peter's, continually holding each other to account for the work they did and the outcomes of the school. Neither was prepared to let the other down and their united front became quite a force.

The school had 175 on roll, now 420 and is moving to two form entry. Staff turnover is low and they are a Schools Direct training school so they 'grow their own' talent. Flexibility has had a part to play in the school's success with both the Deputy Headteacher and Key Stage 1 phase leaders working four days a week. The Year 2 class teachers are a talent partnership (job-share) with PPA time set aside for handover and joint planning. Lynn is clear that a successful class share should be about fitting the competence of the post sharers to the headteacher's and school's criteria. Choosing to be flexible in some circumstances, 'does not have to mean opening the floodgates to everyone. As the headteacher, you decide what will work for your pupils'. In February 2016 Ofsted visited the school and graded it outstanding in all areas. When Ofsted returned in 2021, they judged that the school continued to be outstanding.

While this would not be a model for everyone or in every scenario, ignoring the benefits of flexibility in a system which needs wisdom and experience is foolish. This works for succession planning with headteachers, but would work just as well if someone was stepping up into another responsibility or TLR role and even for class teachers. A number of MATs promote 'buddying' or 'shadowing' a new role or responsibility, before taking it on full time. The ITT process is really flexible and essentially job sharing with more experienced teachers, so why does this disappear as part of our everyday practice once we are qualified? The collaborative, supportive relationship between trained teachers and their professional mentors and coaches is essential to their development and navigation of the first years in the profession. The loss of this collaboration will contribute to the statistic from the 2018 DfE School Workforce census that only 67.7 per cent of trainee teachers are still in service after five years. Continuing the flexibility that allows teachers to draw on the experience and expertise of their 'elders' will help to reduce this figure.

We know that if organisations embed coaching for all staff at all levels, it goes some way towards valuing lifelong learning. However, there are specific needs for roles which you have not yet inhabited and watching someone who is experienced is so incredibly helpful. Watch masters at work, magpie, copy, assimilate into your own practice, reflect. Flexibility and job sharing can formalise these well-trodden and successful methods into our own CPD. The much quoted statistic from a 2013 internal review by Hewlett Packard and the crux of Sandberg's argument in 'Lean In' states that men will apply for a role if they only have experience of 60 per cent of the competencies. Initially put down to lack of confidence, further research by LinkedIn (LinkedIn) and the *Harvard Business Review* shows that both men and women avoid applying for a job for which they do not feel qualified. A lack of understanding of the application process – that there is an expectation you can learn on the job – will go some way towards addressing the leadership imbalance in our schools. In a school where staff were encouraged to learn from someone in a role which interested them for succession planning and individual development, women would not only feel more empowered but more equipped to apply for promotion and take on roles which they previously would not have felt qualified for. In a profession where, according to Paul Whiteman, general secretary of school leaders' union NAHT, we have 'the least experienced teaching workforces in the world', we would benefit from retaining the wisdom and leadership of those who have sustained a lifelong career in the profession. If succession planning is not an option, consider who you are preventing from moving up in your organisation and what a disservice that is to the children you serve. With the retirement age rising and with a lot of energy required for sustaining that level of professionalism and excellence, would we not have smoother handovers and benefit to developing new staff if we offered staff near retirement age the option of staying on flexibly?

It is a similar situation for those who are caring for elderly relatives. These are precious moments with members of their family which they will not be able to have again. Allowing them freedom and flexibility to really take care of their ageing parent, to say goodbye without the stress of the day job is so valuable and so helpful in what can be a very difficult time. Many of those teachers are not ready to leave the profession altogether, but the two roles appear incompatible and so they retire when they could have time out, or a little more flexibility until they are ready to return.

By embracing more flexibility in our employment conditions in schools, we not only allow and encourage those nearing retirement to stay in our schools but we also provide opportunities for much improved succession planning and for newer leaders and teachers to learn invaluable lessons setting them up for success in the future. Effective school leaders create up to three extra months of learning for each student per year (Leaver et al., 2019), so ensuring that our senior leaders get the best possible development will impact positively on student outcomes.

New graduates

Millennials are looking for portfolio careers. According to Timewise, 92 per cent of millennials either already work flexibly or wish they could (Flexible Working: A Talent Imperative, Timewise, 2017). People are more likely to change career over the course of their lifetimes with portfolio and 'slashie' careers becoming increasingly popular (IPSE, 2019). A portfolio career is where someone splits their time between two or more flexible roles and a slashie is someone who lists a number of roles when describing themselves professionally, i.e. 'I'm a teacher/designer/animator'. This has always been popular in creative industries, but the appeal is growing for all ages and particularly among those aged 35 and under. Not only do we need to attract these people to teaching but we should be actively doing so. The skillsets and diversity that they can bring to our classrooms and staffroom hold great advantage for the education sector.

With so many millennials wanting to work flexibly, we are competing with other professions for them. If we make it harder to work flexibly, teaching is less attractive as a career, and it also prevents them from becoming a teacher/author, a teacher/artist, a teacher/statistician or a teacher/sportswoman. If it is all or nothing and the younger generation of teachers choose 'nothing' in terms of working in education, then not only will we have a shortage of teachers coming in but also we will lose valuable experience and variety in the tapestry of diversity in our schools.

The DfE's Recruitment and Retention strategy identifies new teachers as a key area of focus. They hope to address the challenge that 'Teachers at the start of their careers do not always get the support they need to build a successful career, and at the moment, too many end up leaving' (DfE, 2019). There are a number of important strands to supporting and developing early career teachers, but offering flexibility needs to be part of this offer.

Recruitment and retention of new teachers is especially important given the shortages in teacher supply that we have seen in recent years and the continued pressure resulting in higher pupil numbers and larger class sizes. Recruitment numbers for ITT courses do not meet current demand (particularly for physics, maths, modern foreign languages and chemistry); the issue is further intensified by increasing pupil numbers, which are set to continue growing by a further 11 per cent between 2018/2019 and 2023/2024 (Worth, 2020).

Career changers

People who retrain and come from other industries are often surprised by the lack of flexibility in teaching. Katie Waldegrave, CEO of NowTeach - an organisation which trains career changers to move into teaching -says that many of their recruits are not surprised that there is a recruitment and retention crisis in the education sector. New teachers who have worked in other sectors previously are surprised by how inflexible working in schools is because we are very much behind the times. Accelerated somewhat by the coronavirus situation, other industries and organisations had already begun to embrace flexible working and its benefits.

The value and diversity that career changers can add to our school will only be fully realised if we can offer them some of the flexibility they are accustomed to in other sectors.

Case Study 3.5 Now Teach

Now Teach is an organisation which trains and supports people who have already had a career in another industry to become teachers. Their participants have already succeeded in one walk of life, 13 per cent have a PhD, 41 per cent have a master's. Now Teach are seeing flexible work in two different ways. The participants see it from the point of view of being able to compare to other sectors where education is worse than many in terms of flexibility. But also, the option of flexible working may be particularly important for those at this stage of life (their average age is 48), often because caring for ageing parents is just as acute a time of challenge for people as having young children. Also ageing itself; there is a question of energy and not just the ageing process but the sense of time. This may be a time of life when they wish to think of different interests and readjust priorities – there is often a greater sense of perspective and that impacts on work–life blend needs.

Those with health issues

Mental and physical health issues can mean that individuals need or would benefit from more flexibility in their work. We have heard examples from teachers with long-term chronic illness, pregnancy-related issues, cancer treatment, anxiety, depression and menopausal women, all of whom would benefit from some level of flexibility. Leaders who are offering flexibility to everyone create a situation of 'prevention rather than cure'. Schools that are not offering flexibility may be preventing individuals and groups of people from joining their organisation or preventing their current employees from working effectively or at all. Are leaders proactive in listening to the voices of everyone in their schools? If we wait for people to reach a level of vulnerability where they feel a burden and awkward when asking for what they need in terms of working conditions, then quite aside from meeting our obligations under the Equalities Act 2010, we really need to look at ourselves and wonder if our approach is humane.

Case study 3.6 Caroline Powell

Caroline is Head of English. She also suffers from cystic fibrosis and Crohn's disease. She has trained, qualified and developed as a teacher as well as becoming a leader and a mother all while managing her illness. Like many people who live with chronic health issues, she has good times and not so good times, so flexible working allows her to continue doing her job. When she needs to have time off in hospital, she and her department are well versed in the systems that make cover for that period work. They have built a bank of curriculum resources that make cover work easy and effective. At times when Caroline is able to administer her own intravenous medications rather than stay in

(Continued)

hospital, she is still able to and willing to work in school for the middle part of the day. She is ambitious and successful and effective in her role, but without flexibility from her school she would not be able to do it. The school benefits from having her in post despite the concessions required. In addition to the moral obligations and duty of care, they are also expected to make these reasonable adjustments to make her working life accessible due to the Equality Act 2010. There is give and take in the working relationship and it is clear that in return for their flexibility the school have retained an excellent, dedicated, committed middle leader who 'pays them back' in abundance.

The Equality Act 2010 legally protects people from discrimination in the workplace. Under the Equality Act 2010, you are disabled if you have a physical or mental impairment that has a 'substantial' and 'long-term' negative effect on your ability to do normal daily activities. The Equality Act 2010 states that employers should make 'reasonable adjustments' to help disabled employees and job applicants for a range of aspects of recruitment and employment including terms of employment.

Scope, a national charity which campaigns for equality for disabled people, says that most flexible working policies do not cover flexible working as a 'reasonable adjustment', but if an employee asks for flexible working as a reasonable adjustment, they have additional rights under the Equality Act 2010. An employer has a duty to make reasonable adjustments for a disabled person to do the job, but they do not have to agree with all requests for adjustments. However, if flexible working is reasonable and necessary for someone to do their job, then they have to agree. What is 'reasonable' will depend on what the teacher needs and whether the school can accommodate it, but there should be serious consideration made to flexible working requests made by those with disabilities both on a legal and moral basis.

We try to teach our children to be inclusive and value diversity – what better way to do this than to demonstrate it to them? Children with physical disabilities or chronic illness rarely see themselves in books and on TV; how wonderful would it be for them to have teachers with similar disabilities and what a brilliant lesson for everyone in preparing to be part of an inclusive and diverse society.

Those returning to teaching

There are many reasons why teachers or leaders may have taken a break from teaching and many reasons why they may benefit from some flexibility on returning to the classroom or school. Long periods of absence for whatever reason (raising a family, health issues, change in circumstances, relocation), can lead to a lack of confidence on return and some may benefit from easing back in to work rather than going back in full time. Operations, illness and ongoing treatments can all leave ongoing issues that require a gentler reintroduction to work. Sometimes these may be physical impairments or symptoms but equally important are unseen mental considerations which should be accommodated as much as possible. Absence due to health issues can mean that staggered returns are both beneficial and necessary, but a compassionate and flexible reintegration can be helpful for members of staff who have been absent due to bereavement, dealing with family illness or other concerns. Flexible phasing in or out after or before a period of absence can allow teachers and leaders to build confidence, it can make handovers more effective and it may be crucial to their wellbeing and the sustainability of their employment and career over the longer term. Whenever there is a period of absence for whatever reason, leaders should want the return to be as successful as possible not just for the smooth running and future of the school but out of compassion and a duty of care to their employee.

For those who have been absent for a longer period of time, a group known as 'returners', flexibility on return to the classroom may be a requirement or indeed a necessity. A woman who has taken a number of years away from work to raise a family, for example, may wish to work flexibly when returning to paid employment. If, during the time spent away from teaching, people have worked in other industries or for themselves, it is likely that they will have had a great deal more flexibility than the rigid and traditional ways of working we see in many school environments.

> *Thousands of former teachers return to the profession each year, so the transition may be easier than you expect. To make your return to teaching as smooth as possible there's plenty of support available, which includes the Return to Teaching Adviser service for returning languages, maths or physics teachers, information on available teaching vacancies and helpful resources to prepare you to get back into the classroom.*
>
> (DfE, 2020)

The DfE's Teacher Recruitment and Retention Strategy published in 2019 talks about the importance of flexible working for attracting those who are qualified to teach but no longer teaching in our schools. Flexible working is one of the key strategic priorities of this work with the DfE committing to 'support headteachers to adapt to changing demands by helping to transform approaches to flexible working in schools'. Any support package for returners must include making improvements to the flexible working offer in the education sector.

> *Not only is the relative inflexibility of secondary schools having a negative impact on leaving rates, but it is also creating a barrier to re-entry for secondary teachers who wish to return to teaching. Our recent evaluation of the Return to Teaching pilot... identified a lack of part-time and flexible working opportunities as one of the main barriers facing secondary teachers who want to return to the profession.*
>
> (Van den Brande and Worth, 2018)

The benefit to schools of attracting and developing returners in the longer term is surely worth some extra effort in the short term. They may feel lacking in confidence or a bit rusty at first, but they are trained and, in some cases, very experienced teachers. The investment in terms of cost and time in re-developing them into effective teachers is much less than it would be to start from scratch with a brand-new trainee.

There are a whole host of reasons why teachers and school leaders may request flexibility and there are just as many reasons why giving it to them would benefit the individuals, the school and wider society. The need or desire for flexibility is often highly personal and while we have made generalisations here about different groups and how they may benefit from flexibility, the best approach to considering flexible working is on an individual level. Where requests are considered with humanity and long-term strategic thinking, the default position is to make flexibility work for each individual and the school rather than to see it as impossible and an inconvenience. The following chapters will provide advice and practical considerations to make that possible.

Summary

This chapter has described:

- The main reasons why teachers might want or need to work flexibly
- Key features of the different groups of people who may seek flexible working
- How offering these groups more flexibility can benefit them as individuals as well the school and wider society

References

Barr, C., Kommenda, N. and Davies, C. (2019). Gender pay gap: What did we learn this year? Available at: https://www.theguardian.com/world/ng-interactive/2019/apr/05/gender-pay-gap-what-did-we-learn-this-year.

DfE (2019, 27 June). School workforce in England: November 2018.

DfE (2020). Get into Teaching Website, 2020. Available at https://getintoteaching.education.gov.uk/events.

Dunn, H. (2017, 12 January). @ShropshireSBM, a School Business Manager for MTPT Project. Available at: https://www.mtpt.org.uk/family-friendly-schools/family-friendly-schools/.

Flexible Working: A Talent Imperative, Timewise (2017). Available at: https://timewise.co.uk/wp-content/uploads/2019/06/Flexible_working_Talent_Imperative.pdf.

Harvard Business Review: Why women don't apply unless they're 100% qualified. Available at: https://hbr.org/2014/08/why-women-dont-apply-for-jobs-unless-theyre-100-qualified.

IPSE: 320,000 people 'have a second self-employed job' (2019, 23 April). Available at: https://www.ipse.co.uk/ipse-news/news-listing/320-000-people-second-self-employed-job-slashie.html.

Joyce, K., Pabayo, R., Critchley, J. A. and Bambra, C. (2010). Flexible working conditions and their effects on employee health and wellbeing. *Cochrane Database Systematic Review*, 2010(2), CD008009. Published 2010 Feb 17. doi:10.1002/14651858.CD008009.pub2

Leaver, C., Lemnos, R. and Scur, D. (2019). Measuring and explaining management in schools: new approaches using public data center for Economic Performance Discussion Paper No. 1656.

LinkedIn: Gender Insights Report. Available at: https://business.linkedin.com/content/dam/me/business/en-us/talent-solutions-lodestone/body/pdf/Gender-Insights-Report.pdf.

NFER (2015). Available at: https://www.nfer.ac.uk/publications/LFSA01/LFSA01.pdf.

Nicks, L., Burd, H. and Barnes, J. (March, 2019). Flexible working qualitative analysis Organisations' experiences of flexible working arrangements. *Behavioural Insights Team*. Available at: https://getintoteaching.education.gov.uk/explore-my-options/return-to-teachingGovernment Equalities Office.

Policy Exchange (2016). Available at: https://policyexchange.org.uk/wp-content/uploads/2016/09/the-Importance-of-Teachers.pdf.

Sandberg, S. and Scovell, N. (2013). *Lean In: Women, Work, and the Will to Lead*. New York, NY: Alfred A. Knopf.

Scope Available at: https://www.scope.org.uk/advice-and-support/work-careers/flexible-working/.

TeacherTapp (2017). Available at: http://teachertapp.co.uk/2017/10/teachers-tapped-week-7/x.

Timewise Foundation (2017). Flexible working: A talent imperative. A research study into the UK Workforce: Who wants flexibility, for what reasons, and how much it matters to them, p.6.

Van den Brande, J. and Worth, J. (2018, 19 July). Part-time teaching: what can secondary schools learn from the most flexible schools? Available at: https://www.nfer.ac.uk/news-events/nfer-blogs/part-time-teaching-what-can-secondary-schools-learn-from-the-most-flexible-schools/.

Wooley, C. (2020). *The Lost Girls*. Melton: John Catt. Available at: https://www.gov.uk/government/statistics/school-workforce-in-england-november-2018.

Worth, J. (2020). *Teacher Labour Market in England: Annual Report 2020*. Slough: NFER.

4

TYPES OF FLEXIBLE WORKING

In this chapter we will:

- Explore the various types of flexible working
- Address historic barriers to flexible working and why there are often failed attempts at flexible working
- Advise on planning for successful flexible working
- Explain why different types of flexibility lead to genuinely inclusive teaching

Introduction

The Chartered Institute for Professional Development (CIPD) is the professional body for those working in HR. They define flexible working as 'arrangements which allow employees to vary the amount, timing, or location of their work' (CIPD, 2020): essentially flexible working is having flexibility in when, how much and where you work. With that definition, it is easy to see how schools have fallen so far behind other sectors as we generally have a fixed working location, and there are prescribed times of the day when teachers and leaders are 'service user facing'. However, this does not make flexibility impossible and all education staff can consider a level of flexible working, regardless of their role in the organisation. In this chapter, we will explore the types of flexibility which are available, and how best to match these with the school context in order to maximise the potential of staff and students.

Types of flexibility

This is not an exhaustive list, but covers the main types of flexible working suitable for an education setting:

- Full time with time off site (remote working)
- PPA time clustered together and off site (remote working)
- Talent partnerships (job-shares)
- Compressed hours
- Staggered hours
- Time off in lieu
- Personal days
- Part-time

Matching context and flexibility

Recognising this variety of options is the first requirement if school leaders are to make positive steps towards a more flexible culture. Understanding that a range of options is available and being able to offer alternatives to the most requested 'part-time' and talent partnership (job-share) options may well be the key to retaining teachers as well as balancing the needs of the school. Even without the large or centralised HR department afforded to larger MATs, it is possible for headteachers and leaders to consider the types of flexibility which are most compatible with their context. Developing flexibility in line with core values and vision of the organisation is the key to maximising the potential of staff, identifying skills gaps and having the most positive outcomes for pupils. Like everything in education, the school context is key to the possibility and potential for flexible working. We advocate moving away from a reactive model in which school leaders accommodate individual requests, to a model where flexibility is woven into the fabric of the school vision and offered to all staff annually. The first stage of achieving this process is to marry up the school vision, values and priorities, with the types of flexibility a school can offer. Consider the scenarios below:

1. The school priority is developing improved literacy. This requires the delivery of daily, intensive phonics intervention. This would need to be delivered daily and consistently by specialist teachers, particularly at secondary level. This might mean that the school's flexible commitment can be to staggered hours (late starts or early finishes), rather than whole days off.
2. The school priority is developing a bespoke CPD programme for all staff. This requires staff to seek out their own, remote CPD at evenings and weekends in order to meet their specific, individual needs. This might mean that the organisation's flexible commitment can be to staff leaving with pupils at the end of the day rather than staying on site for meetings.
3. The school priority is developing student wellbeing. This requires delivery of a varied programme of extra-curricular activities for all children in the morning to get pupils ready

for learning. This might mean that the school's flexible commitment can be earlier finishes or time off in lieu.

4. The school priority is retaining a high-quality, inclusive staff body with up-to-date industry knowledge. This requires ability to attract career changers, or people who can continue working in industry as well as teaching. This might mean that the school's flexible commitment would be to offer a variety of types of flexibility and review this annually with all staff.
5. The school priority is developing more positive relationships with parents and carers. This requires primary teaching staff to be available for face-to-face contact and conversations at the end of every day. This might mean that the school's flexible commitment can be later starts or remote PPA time at the start of the school day. At secondary level, it requires more regular contact with home for a smaller group of students. This might be achieved by widening the pool of staff (beyond teaching staff) who are form tutors and who register the children. This might mean that the school's flexible commitment is personal days, or remote PPA time all at once in the middle of the day.
6. The trust's priority is substantial pastoral support and strong links with outside agencies. This requires time, expertise and dedication of more than one person per year group. This might mean that the organisation's commitment is to well-prepared talent partnerships (job-shares) for key pastoral roles. Consideration would be given to how the week is divided and how continuity is maintained from Friday to Monday.
7. The school priority is a varied performance art and music programme. This requires dedicated and specialist staff to coach and support students in advance of and during performances. This might mean the school's flexible commitment will be to annualised hours to adequately remunerate for the extra time put into performances or that staff involved in these productions and performances are offered time off in lieu.

Whatever the priorities and vision of the organisation, it is preferable to have considered the types of flexibility which are most suited in your context, both in terms of what you are able to offer and what you are trying to achieve. This list is likely to evolve as the needs of the school change; however, it is a much stronger starting point than reacting to individual requests from members of staff, especially as these requests tend to be based purely on what they have seen before rather than creative thinking. Ideally, as part of their annual and longer-term planning, headteachers would align potential opportunities for flexible working with the priorities and vision of the school. This would allow for the kind of fruitful conversations which retain staff such as, 'I can offer this type of flexibility now, and next academic year, we are looking to do X, which will mean an additional type of flexible arrangement is available'. It also allows for much more sustainable staffing because headteachers would be able to offer regular, 'on-the-job' responsibility to staff above their current role who are covering for a flexible lead post for a short period of time each week.

Practicalities and logistics

There are still logistical concerns from headteachers and leaders about how to manage a flexible staff body. These concerns tend to be about communication, timetabling and accountability. The concerns tend to be around how to effectively manage teachers on different contracts. It is totally feasible, and we have examples of schools which already offer a variety of working contracts each academic year. One of the benefits outlined in Chapter 3 was that offering flexible working demonstrates trust in your staff. The staff body feel trusted if they are allowed elements of flexibility which fit in with their lifestyle and allow them to be the best they can be. Trust your staff and trust your systems. For example, consider the weekly whole staff briefing; Lucy worked for a whole school year with a late start on a Monday. In those pre-COVID times, it was 'impossible' and 'unthinkable' that there would be any way to join that briefing remotely, so instead she read the whole staff e-mail which was always sent round as an accompaniment or back up to the briefing itself. In the Autumn Term 2020, no school would be able to safely hold an in-person whole staff briefing, and many schools adapted their practice. Staff across the country could be seen listening to announcements while also fulfilling other duties which everyone has on a Monday morning. Some schools did away with the briefing altogether and reduced whole school communication to a one-pager/presentation per week which staff could read at a time convenient to them. There might be some protestations at the loss of a whole community event, but if the purpose of the briefing is to relay information, there are effective methods of completing a whole staff briefing flexibly and remotely.

It was a similar scenario with core hours and whole staff CPD. Schools up and down the country were in a bizarre situation where departments or the whole school were meeting remotely while individuals were on site, but not allowed in the same physical space. Spread out in classrooms all around the school, without the benefit of face-to-face interaction. This created an opportunity to try something previously considered 'impossible': allowing staff to leave the site and join the meeting from a location of their choice rather than being isolated in a classroom participating remotely with colleagues who were in the next room. This was eminently preferable and made no difference to staff involvement or commitment. Contributing while commuting outside of rush hour traffic, being early to pick up their own children, running on the treadmill, walking in the daylight before the darkness descended again at 4 pm: the value and effect of these experiences are difficult to quantify, until you measure the impact on the children being taught by these teachers.

In order to manage these logistics, we make four recommendations:

1. Align commitment to types of flexibility with the priorities of your organisation. (see Chapter 6 for more detail)
2. Ask each staff member annually how they would like to work.
3. Offer specific contract types, or individual contracts depending on the needs of the school and staff body.
4. Trial and refine.

Sharing the various possibilities with staff will be necessary so that they choose the correct model for themselves and their circumstances. You might also need to share the types of questions staff should ask themselves before making their decision. Is their commute hampered by traffic? Is the drop off to nursery too tight? Do they have a favourite gym class they never want to miss? Is their ageing parent more lucid in the early morning? In spite of the fear of the 'floodgates' opening and a high volume of staff requesting to work 0.8 with Fridays off, this is rarely requested and demonstrates a misunderstanding of the teaching workforce. Teachers already have chunks of holiday time throughout the year, so a three-day weekend is not the desired pinnacle seen in other sectors. Headteachers are almost always pleasantly surprised by how easy it is to accommodate individual preferences from each staff member when they consult the whole staff body. No one teacher is asking too much, and many will ask for no flexibility at all. Finding out what staff would ideally like, allows a school to make a decision about what to do next. We have case studies of schools which accommodate each and every request on an individual basis. Others look at the needs of staff and offer three or four different types of contract. Whatever you decide, the flexibility you offer should suit your school context and your staff body.

Case Study 4.1 Cleo de Jong, Secondary Assistant Headteacher

Cleo de Jong is an Assistant Headteacher at a secondary school in North-West London.

All staff at my school can request flexible working arrangements. This ranges from SLT who are given leave to attend their child's sports day or the first day at school, to TAs who need additional time to do the school drop off. The restrictive nature of the school day means that once a child moves from nursery to primary school, it is impossible to do a drop off and get to school on time, particularly when no breakfast club is available at the child's new school. I am able to start the school day at 9am, allowing for a stress-free morning. The hours and duties missed are reassigned to a different time during the day, for example, in the form of an extra lesson taught or an extra afterschool detention covered.

The benefits of this approach for me personally are that a relaxed family breakfast can be eaten at home and not in the car or in a draughty school hall. The additional time I spend with my young family in the morning goes some way to compensate for the frequent late evenings that often occur in school life.

The school benefits from increased discretionary effort shown by staff in general and SLT in particular. Clear value is demonstrated by the school to family commitments and as a result, staff show a strong commitment to the school. We have a very low staff turnover with flexible working arrangements and onsite nursery provision quoted as a major factor in why many staff choose to stay.

The low turnover means that pupils benefit from consistency of staff year on year. In the instance of compressed hours, their class teacher is made more available for more periods than previously allocated by the timetable. They also see a flexible approach to leadership modelled in their school community, which broadens their perspective on working life.

Leaders often have non-negotiables for their professional life but having non-negotiables for your personal life is just as important. Making a request with the most optimistic expectations in mind allows a compromise to be found that suits both you and the school.

Full time with time off site (remote working)

This is where a member of staff will be contracted to work full time, but will work part of that time remotely off site. This arrangement might be a regular weekly occurrence or at specific times of the school year for particular tasks. It is especially useful for SLT staff with lower teaching timetables to spend time on tasks which require uninterrupted attention which is often sadly lacking in a typical school day. It has the succession planning advantage of providing opportunities for second in charge or more junior members of staff to take on middle or senior leadership responsibility while the post holder is away from the school site.

PPA time all at once and off site (remote working)

This is where a member of staff will not be required to remain in school during their PPA time and/or that PPA time will be deliberately grouped together allowing them to work for a more sustained period remotely off site. This has the added benefit of being offered to both full time and flexible working staff. Teachers can then use this block of time in a way which best suits them. They have a choice to complete all their required PPA at that specific time, or to complete PPA in the evenings and utilise this bonus daytime slot for something completely different. Examples include teachers taking a specific gym class, singing in a choir, bird watching, seeing an exhibition, doing their weekly shop while the supermarket is empty, volunteering at a food bank and dropping their own kids at school. This affords a level of freedom usually absent in a traditional teaching timetable and the perceived 'gift' has an immensely positive impact on a teacher's productivity when they are back on site. It is a relatively small concession with minimal impact on the rest of the staff body. Where it is afforded to everyone, all staff begin to see the value in this time and are happy to support while others are off site. This is especially useful for more experienced teaching staff who are working flexibly as they do not require as much PPA time or respite in between lessons as an early career teacher.

Talent partnerships (job-shares)

Talent Partnerships (job-shares) can be used for any role in an organisation and can add immense value and energy. Unfortunately, in education they often have a bad press for two significant reasons. The first is that they are rarely set up with the same kind of precision planning expected of a whole school structure or system. Most job-shares come about because there are two people choosing to work fewer hours for similar or vastly different reasons. It seems like a perfect solution and, logistically, it is. However, a job-share requires mature skills which need to be honed and worked upon if the role is to be carried out successfully. This brings us to the second big issue, which is semantics: names matter. The term 'job-share' is wholly inadequate and often holds connotations of failure from previous, poorly planned experience. The truth is that, when it works well, this is a far more advanced and technical solution than two people sharing a job. It is a collaboration of the skills and attributes of two people in a role which benefits from their combined experience and expertise. It is much more than simply sharing the tasks involved in completing a job: it is a 'talent partnership'. We first heard this phrase coined by Sara Horsfall on her job-sharing platform Ginibee (Horsfall, 2017). Sara is in the process of developing 'Partner Up and Teach' which formalises the partnering of teachers and leaders in roles at all levels. This is a platform which the DfE have had on the agenda for a long time. The Civil Service actually already have an amazing job-share platform which has been running for years and job-shares there are commonplace. When Lucy began looking for alternatives to full-time leadership, she assumed that there was a platform which would link her with someone with a similar set of expertise and values. A simple, centralised way to find someone in her area with similar level of experience with whom she would be able build a working partnership and apply for roles. However, apart from a few well documented examples of shared headship, there was nothing. Since then, organisations like The Shared Headship Network have helped create a space where partnerships can flourish and we have used our own network to partner up individuals who have successfully secured senior leader and headteacher roles together. Vicky Brooks and Kirsten Kennedy contacted us looking for a way to continue working in education. We used our Twitter following to partner them up and they are now co-headteachers in Leicestershire. Read their story on page 94, and if you are interested in this model, start by referring to it as a talent partnership rather than a job-share: you will feel more positive about it already. Next, turn to Chapter 7 which is dedicated to maximising the potential of talent partnerships.

Compressed hours

This might be working full-time hours but over four days rather than five. Last year for example, Lindsay taught a 0.8 timetable compressed into three days on site. Knowledge of school context and staff experience and capability is crucial if planning to allow compressed hours. While it might not be suitable for a trainee to have all their teaching back-to-back and PPA off site, for an experienced teacher, it may suit both them and the organisation very well. Experienced senior leaders might also complete their role in four days on site. SLT with experience can often do the job in less time; giving them the opportunity to work fewer hours to pursue other interests saves the school money. This is also an ideal scenario for more senior leaders who are closer to retirement as it allows the school to retain their expertise for a lower cost and ensures sustainable staffing by allowing less experienced colleagues to cover the post holder while they are off site.

Staggered hours

In many schools, LSAs/TAs work on contracts with slightly altered break and lunch times, so schools already have staff on staggered hours contracts. This can include arrangements of later starts, earlier finishes, extended or different lunch and break times. These can be offered to full or part-time staff. The school has a legal, safeguarding responsibility to take registers and to have a sufficient ratio of staff to students on site, so there is a limit on how many staff can access later starts or earlier finishes at one time. Where demand is high, schools can aim to offer several late starts to each staff member throughout half a term, or to particular staff on a weekly or fortnightly basis. For example, one day per week/fortnight can be valuable respite for staff involved in pastoral roles which often require intervention at the end of each school day. This helps with succession planning, as colleagues can try on-the-job training by taking on responsibilities of the post holder in their absence. Another option is to consider whether it is always necessary for a teaching member of staff to take the register and morning form time. Involving admin and site staff in these roles can have a positive impact on the school community as well as opening up levels of flexibility for all those working in the school building. The third example, as mentioned earlier in this chapter, is of a school prioritising student wellbeing by providing a regular and varied programme for all students. If this takes place first thing in the morning, it would allow for a whole staff rota of staggered starts. If all pupils begin the day in extra-curricular spaces of yoga, choir, running, etc, then specialist staff can be deployed to larger numbers of children. The programme rotates, so do the staff required on site, and registration takes place at these larger group sessions, meaning that not all staff are required on site until lessons begin.

Time off in lieu

This can be offered where staff work extra days in the holidays, or late evenings. This might be for all school staff, for example, a late start on an INSET day in lieu of an extra open evening. It might be for specific individuals like those who work in the lead up to GCSE/A Level results day getting a day off in lieu at a time of their choosing. Another example is for someone who works flexibly, but attends training/parents evening/INSET on their non-school day who then gets to take an additional day off at another time in the year. Days off in lieu demonstrate recognition of the above and beyond effort offered willingly by staff but which is not remunerated or written into their contract. It allows the school to deploy staff at the times they are needed most while appreciating staff commitment and strengthening their loyalty.

Annualised hours

This is where an employee works a certain number of hours over the year but there is some flexibility about when they work. This might be used for drama and music teachers who need to work more hours at certain times of the year for school productions or (indeed?) for any staff who are required for more hours at certain times of the year, for example, in the run up to exams. Similar to days off in lieu, annualised hours recognise the ebb and flow of workload for specific roles and supports those teachers whose specialisms insist that they experience intensive, committed periods of work with students.

Remote working

We are all much more familiar with the possibilities of remote working since the COVID-19 pandemic and the experience of lockdown. Tools and technology were utlised by staff and students which might previously have been ignored and, while there is general agreement that the most effective learning experience for most students is in a classroom, there is a place for remote working in education which would not have been entertained previously. This can be as simple as not requiring staff to be on site during their PPA time or it could be SLT working from home for part of the week. It might be online mentoring meetings or dialling in to meetings/briefings. In particular circumstances, teachers may deliver content to pupils remotely: if the students or teachers are well, but isolating, lessons can be attended virtually. Where members of staff change role or school during the school year, they may still deliver remotely to their former classes preparing for exams. In these cases, the teacher has formed a strong relationship with the students, and there would be less impact on the learning if the same teacher delivers remotely, rather than expecting a new teacher to do so. Remote working is any time you are working but not physically on the school site.

Personal days

These can be offered to both full-time and flexible working staff and are known as mental health days, family days, Christmas shopping days, duvet days etc. They recognise that although holiday time is valuable and valued, paid time off during term time offers possibilities which the traditional school timetable does not allow. We know examples of schools who offer an option for staff to begin the summer holiday early if their absence rate is low and their attendance is 100 per cent. This can be an extremely generous reward if a member of staff travels abroad to see family over the longer holidays and is allowed to book flights which are cheaper than the peak holiday cost. If rewarding staff attendance in the same way as pupils does not fit with your context, occasional paid time off is always welcome. Staff can use it to attend medical appointments, attend their own children's nativity plays, pursue an interest or hibernate under the covers on a dark midwinter day. It is wise to make this a policy for all staff as this can prevent resentment of groups like parents. If afforded to all staff, it has the benefit of reducing absenteeism overall and demonstrates a reward for hard work and commitment, for going over and above timetabled hours.

Part-time

Although part-time arrangements are the most common type of flexibility offered to teachers, they are not the most creative solution and, given the options available, colleagues may choose flexibility already mentioned over the more traditional working part time. It is possible that a part-time working pattern is chosen because it is all that has been experienced, and not because it is the most effective solution. We regularly state that semantics matter, and are on the hunt for a replacement for the woefully inadequate label of 'part-time'. The term is often synonymous with part-committed: you never get as much out of a part-time member of staff. As it is often the most common type of flexibility offered and not necessarily executed with much thought, it can have the reputation of being troublesome, time-consuming and 'difficult'. Once we move beyond logistics, the students benefit from the teacher's breaks in between the intensive mental gymnastics of a school timetable allowing for reflection, focus on other interests and a return to the workplace with renewed energy and rigour. We do need to be mindful that 'part-time' staff often work more hours to compensate than their full-time counterparts and add immense value to an organisation at the detriment of their own wellbeing.

Teachers tend to work part-time for one of two reasons. Either the hours of a full-time post do not allow the brain space for other interests and activities. Alternatively, a full-time post does not appear to be compatible with putting their family (young children, aging relatives and everything in between) into a box for the weekend and the holidays when they have head space to give them their full attention. Something leaders should ask themselves is: why do so many staff request part-time as opposed to other types of flexible working? It might be due to a lack of awareness or, unfortunately more often, it may arise from the view that it simply is not possible to work 'in a school like mine' without putting in a huge amount of 'overtime'. Staff requesting to work part time ought to be given a safe space similar to an exit interview to be asked why. Failure to do this inevitably means that schools are saved from having transparent conversations about workload. It demonstrates a celebration of the 'martyr' teacher mentality in which only something life-changing such as having a new baby or a dying relative will allow you to assess your workload and realise that what is being asked of you is too much. This is not a model which organisations should aspire to.

We regularly receive communication from individuals planning to request a part-time position because of issues with completing their workload. In many schools, it is still the outdated perception that a TLR or leadership post cannot be performed on anything other than a full-time basis, and so individuals are forced to step down in order to manage their workload rather than the school tackling the workload issue head on. Individuals sacrifice career and development in order to keep doing a job they love but at a capacity they can sustain. It is incredibly important both for the school and the individual that no one is deciding to go 'part-time' to solve an issue of workload. If you are planning to go part-time because of this, or if you have staff requesting part-time for this reason, you will not be alone, and there needs to be bigger questions asked about the organisation itself. While there may be other demands made on staff time which they wish to accommodate with flexible working, they should not need to reduce their working hours to be able to complete the minimum expectations of their role on their 'days off'.

We know, anecdotally, that this happens a lot. Individuals can see that they will be unable to cope with the time demands of the job and that, rather than discuss those demands, it feels easier to request a reduction in hours to complete the tasks required by the school. This is not helpful for anyone, but it is understandable as much of the individual's internal narrative at this point may be around not being able to manage, or not coping, and so it is easier to see the fault with oneself than with the organisation. If circumstances have dictated a change in ability to complete workload, it is also rarely the right time for an individual to be spearheading a conversation about workload which might not apply to the majority of the organisation. This might not be voiced by others because the majority of staff have circumstances which allow for the type of commitment and 'martyr' teacher hours which we all remember from our trainee years but which are unsustainable long term. We know that teachers always do more than their contracted hours and repeated studies by the Trades Union Congress (TUC) show teachers putting in more hours of 'overtime' than other dedicated sectors such as medical staff or the police. This suggests that it is this 'overtime' which has to be stripped back once there is something in a teacher's life which has to take priority. If we are able to be wedded to the job, with little time for anything else, workload is manageable, but a change in circumstances would make that type of commitment impossible.

Now we are clear on what part-time should not be used for, then part-time should be an opportunity for staff members to work fewer hours and with a reduced timetable across the week. This is a particularly effective model for schools looking for specialist teachers or teachers of shortage subjects, and it suits teachers who have other interests or commitments. It is also useful for parents at particular times in their own children's lives, or if teachers are 'sandwich' carers for both their children and their parents. For most, working part-time is for a particular, limited time-period. Supporting teachers and leaders at these often vulnerable times is crucial to keeping significant numbers of teachers in the classroom, and in the profession. Working part-time allows individuals to maintain their classroom expertise and subject knowledge and ensures that students have an effective teacher in the classroom. Depending on the arrangement, the staff member may contribute in the same way as other members of staff: sharing a pastoral group, communicating with parents and carers and attending INSET days. Part-time might mean simply paying a subject specialist for their teaching time and demanding nothing more from them than marking, planning and delivery of lessons to specific groups of students. Holly Power set up her organisation 'Return to Teach' while working as a member of SLT and raising her two small boys. She was "sick of seeing so many good people leave the profession" and set up a remarkably simple subscription service which cost the school much less than a supply or cover agency and was free for teachers. Schools were able to pay a music or A Level Physics specialist for their teaching hours, and the teacher was rewarded with a role which played to their strengths, and allowed them to pursue other interests.

The more traditional part-time working afforded to teachers usually translates to the demands of a full-time role, but on a pro rata basis. A lot of anxiety is alleviated on both sides if these logistical details are considered by the employer in advance. For example with attendance of INSET days, consider whether you need all of your staff to attend all of these, in which case you will need to offer to pay overtime for the days they are not contracted to work. Alternatively, you may wish them to attend at the start of the year only, and then attend INSET days pro rata based on their days working in school. If someone works 0.6 and there are 5 INSET days over a school year, the arrangement could be that they attend the first two and one other which is most appropriate for their level of experience or role. Attendance of evening and non-working day events should have the same consideration. Be clear whether you require a part-time member of staff to attend an evening event on their non-teaching day, and support them where possible. For example, it might be possible for the children of staff to attend the same crèche facility which is being provided for younger siblings while parents have meetings with teachers. Similarly, performance management systems need to ensure that employees are able to be assessed and awarded performance related pay within the contracted hours that they work. It is an HR responsibility to check whether staff working part-time are given sufficient time to plan for formal observations and that the timescales of performance management are fair. While part-time has been a staple for schools for many years, it is very likely that other types of flexible working will suit your context and your staff much better.

Teaching and learning responsibilities (TLRs)

It is worth thinking carefully about TLRs for employees working flexibly and taking each situation on its merits. Depending on the type of flexible working arrangement, a school might not be able to insist that the full TLR is completed on pro rata pay. If an employee is reducing their hours, their TLR might need to be reduced or shared among other members of the team. However, if an employee is simply working off site, or compressed hours, they will still be responsible for and should be remunerated for the full TLR. These conversations should be free and open in order to ascertain the employee's preference. The solution will be different if they are requesting flexible working because the post and workload is currently unmanageable. If this is the case, it might be better to divide up the responsibilities of the TLR without the member of staff having to work part-time. This ensures that the workload is shared, that staff are supported and will alleviate concerns the employee had about completing the TLR, without having to reduce their contact time in school. Consider why the TLR is unmanageable and how it can be broken down. There are elements of most roles which it is easy to divide up and which might play to the strengths of the team, rather than being over reliant on an individual. If middle leaders and SLT have a good and sensible idea about job design and the demands of TLR posts, most of these issues can be resolved easily. With all contractual issues, resolving what seems like the smallest of issues can alleviate stress for all parties.

Whatever flexibility you can offer as a school and whatever staff decide, it is worth considering that flexibility does not have to be long term. Many of the anxieties staff have around returning to work after a significant break might be alleviated if the school allows flexibility for the first few weeks or months after they return. A phased return can be a really positive way of settling in to the new routine. By allowing employees time to adjust, you might be able to keep them in your school and in the profession for a lot longer than if they have to commit to a particular pattern of working for the entirety of the next academic year. There are times in life when people will need more flexibility and these times cannot always be neatly boxed off. Medical appointments of any kind do not always fall during school holidays, and intensive treatment for often invisible needs becomes a temporary priority for the individual. It is times like these when a little flexibility and humanity would avoid losing those teachers altogether. If we come to be known as a sector which can manage this side of an employee's life, we might begin to encourage people in who would never have considered teaching.

Case Study 4.2 Caroline Biddle, Teacher

Caroline Biddle kindly shared with us what her fertility IVF fertility treatment journey was like. Now that her son is around, she has had "plenty of best moments, but navigating fertility treatment around life and work was heinous". Research into fertility in the workplace by FNUK and Middlesex University indicates that 50 per cent of the participants would have needed more than a week off work during a cycle of IVF. In other sectors, employees can navigate this using a set amount of paid annual leave, or make up the hours working from home. On difficult days, there is the option to sit quietly away from others, but as we know and Caroline explains, in teaching it is 'all or nothing'. Fertility treatment can consist of necessary and unavoidable; consultations, pre-screening, medication, scans, further medication, egg retrieval, fertilisation and phone calls with updates from the embryologist, add on treatments, mock transfers, embryo transfer and the 2-week wait where women are asked not to test and wait to find out if the embryo has implanted with the lining of the uterus. During this process, "IVF affected me not just socially, but financially, emotionally and mentally. Sometimes teaching was a great distraction from treatment, but other times it became an obstruction."

Infertility and IVF bring a lot of trauma that the member of staff might not be prepared for. As well as going through the process itself, there are concerns about; who else knows, whether it is having an impact on how you are perceived for promotion or career development, and guilt for giving colleagues extra, last minute work when these appointments occur during term time.

Caroline felt "vulnerable" and often went into work following difficult appointments, when she probably should have been at home, because she did not want to look as though she was taking advantage of the situation. Caroline has set up 'Fertility Issues in

Teaching' to help raise awareness of how a little flexibility in schools could make the whole process easier to manage. It is difficult enough with children asking whether you are pregnant because you are swollen from hormone injections, so her practical suggestions include:

- an equitable and inclusive IVF policy that is not too prescriptive
- encourage staff to not return to school following appointments if they're not in the right frame of mind, or, offer an hour's grace to adjust in a quiet space on returning to school
- do not ask for proof of appointments: believe us.
- scrap the absence request form – this is not a dentist appointment
- have fertility awareness training to better understand how to communicate with staff going through fertility struggles. This will avoid asking the member of staff to explain the IVF process to you and prevent you from offering any unwanted advice.
- offer reduced timetable/days
- support staff to speak to a counsellor
- encourage fertility support networks for staff
- please do not suggest adoption – yes we have considered it and no it's not for us at this moment in time

Most schools promote equality of opportunity in their vision and values statement, and we would ask: if you do not offer flexibility, how can you say that you are modelling those values? We know that the teaching workforce is disproportionately female and, while caring responsibilities remain predominantly with women, lack of flexibility will negatively influence their working life and their career progression. There are many factors at play which explain why teaching is not a workforce which reflects society. An example is in Primary, where outdated preconceptions about the capability or predisposition of men especially to Early Years teaching mean that teaching does not welcome everyone. Flexible working is not a silver bullet, but it might open up the profession to people who had not previously considered it and it is one way to break these barriers for everyone to ensure that teaching is a genuinely inclusive profession.

We want teachers who have time for other interests, who feel trusted as to when and how they complete their professional work. We are bound by the needs of the school and the 'service user facing' nature of the job. We know from this informal and unplanned 'experiment' of lockdown learning that, while there might be some advantages for some students, the gap is widening and the mental load is heavy. In short: there is no substitute for an effective teacher in their classroom teaching kids with whom they have built excellent relationships. For this reason, we need teachers to be in school during those core hours, but we can be creative about how this is managed to maximise the energy and potential of every member of staff. In many schools, it is still considered lacking in commitment if staff walk out with the children at the end of the day. In these schools where teachers feel most trusted, this should not be an issue.

As a leader, I should know that whatever my staff member is leaving to do that day is going to have an impact on their wellbeing and, in turn, an impact on the children they teach. Offering even a small element of flexibility to all staff as standard will make staff feel trusted and empowered, which they will reward with productivity and loyalty to the school.

Summary

This chapter has described:

- The link between context and types of flexibility
- The most common types of flexible working suited to education
- Examples of how schools are using flexible working effectively
- Why offering flexible working helps you to be a more inclusive workplace

References

CIPD (2020). Flexible working toolkit. Available at: www.cipd.co.uk/knowledge/fundamentals/relations/flexible-working/hr-toolkit. www.cipd.co.uk/Images/how-to-evaluate-flexible-working_tcm18-72165.pdf.

CIPD (2021). Flexible working practices factsheet. Available at: www.cipd.co.uk/knowledge/fundamentals/relations/flexible-working/factsheet#gref.

Coalter, M. (2018). *Talent Architects: How to Make Your School a Great Place to Work*. Melton: John Catt Educational.

Exploring Flexible Working Practice in Schools Report. The Department for Education. Available at: www.gov.uk/government/publications/exploring-flexible-working-practice-in-schools.

Gibson, C., de Menezes, L. M. and Kelliher, C. (2020). Flexible working and performance: A systematic review of the evidence for a business case. *International Journal of Management Reviews*, 13(4), 452–74.

Horsfall, S. (2017, 14 November). Ginibee®: Introducing talent partnerships. Available at: www.linkedin.com. www.linkedin.com/pulse/ginibee-introducing-talent-partnerships-sara-horsfall/ (accessed 30 June 2021).

NFER (2019). Part time teaching and flexible working in schools. Available at: www.nfer.ac.uk/media/3476/part-time_teaching_and_flexible_working_in_secondary_schools.pdf.

Trade Union Congress (2019). Workers in the UK put in more than £32 billion worth of unpaid overtime last year' TUC analysis. Available at: www.tuc.org.uk/news/workers-uk-put-more-ps32-billion-worth-unpaid-overtime-last-year-tuc-analysis.

5

FLEXIBLE WORKING REQUESTS

In this chapter we will:

- Outline legal and statutory issues relating to flexible working in schools
- Consider flexible working policies
- Discuss how to make and deal with flexible working requests

Introduction

When current employees want to work more flexibly, they may make a flexible working request. This might be after a period of parental leave, a change in circumstances or due to health or age-related needs. Flexible working is a way of working that suits an employee's needs, for example, working part-time, having flexible start and finish times, or working from home. Making a formal request for flexible working is also known as 'making a statutory application'. All employees have the right to make a flexible working request if they have been an employee of the organisation for the last 26 weeks. Individuals can only make one flexible working request in any 12-month period.

On 30 June 2014, the Flexible Working Regulations 2014 (Regulations) came into force expanding flexible working rights for employees in England, Scotland and Wales. From a school's perspective flexible working requests can be difficult to process and agree. Particularly the first few times a request is made, it can be hard to navigate the system and understand what the legal issues and requirements are.

Dealing with flexible working requests

Schools must deal with requests in a 'reasonable manner'. If an employer does not handle a request in a reasonable manner, the employee can take them to an employment tribunal.

Dealing with a request in a reasonable manner may include:

- assessing the advantages and disadvantages of each individual application (it is not acceptable to have a blanket policy of 'no flexible working')
- holding a meeting to discuss the request with the employee (this can be in person or a phone/video call and should be private)
- allowing employees to be accompanied by a work colleague to any meetings or appeal discussions. The employee should be informed about this prior to the discussion.
- offering an appeal process
- not discriminating unlawfully against the employee
- making it clear what information employees should include in their request
- conveying the decision as soon as possible
- dealing with requests within a period of three months from first receipt, unless you agree to extend this period with the employee

ACAS's Code of Practice for Handling Requests in a Reasonable Manner (ACAS, 2014) provides more details. In the event of an employment tribunal, these will be taken into account when considering relevant cases.

Possible outcomes of a flexible working request

When an employee makes a statutory request for flexible working, there are three possible outcomes: (1) The request is accepted, (2) The request is accepted but with modifications or (3) The request is rejected.

1. Accept the request
   Schools do not need to hold a meeting to discuss the application if you intend to grant the request as is. The school should write to the employee outlining the agreed changes and the date they will start from. The terms and conditions in the employee's contract should also be amended.
2. Accept the request with modifications
   The meeting should be used as an opportunity to discuss and explore the request. School leaders should weigh the possible costs against potential benefits and these discussions may be an opportunity to explore ways to mitigate any issues and determine mutually agreed terms. If a compromise can be agreed, the school should write to the employee outlining the changes and the start date and amend the employee's contract accordingly.

Case Study 5.1 Sherish Osman, Flexible Working Request

When Sherish was on maternity leave with her second child, she made an application for flexible working. After her first maternity leave, she returned to work full time in her role as

English Teacher and Lead Teacher (working with and observing other teachers and improving whole school teaching and learning). With support and encouragement from The Maternity Teacher Paternity Teacher Project (MTPT) and Flexible Teacher Talent, she put together her application. It was positive and highlighted the benefits of her proposed arrangement of working a 0.8 contract with three days in school and one at home, but it also addressed some of the potential implications for the school. The school met with her and discussed the proposals. There was some concern from the senior leadership team that because her leadership role involved so much observation and other work with staff in the classroom that it would not be possible to do remotely. After considering her request the school offered her two alternatives, a 0.8 contract as Lead Teacher or a 0.6 contract as an English Teacher. They were not able to accommodate her request due to the nature of the leadership role but they offered some other ways to work flexibly.

Sherish decided to work 0.6 as an English Teacher and give up her leadership role but her Deputy Head contacted her a few weeks later to say they had changed their minds and wanted to accept her original request of 0.8 Lead Teacher with one day working from home. The Head and Deputy Head had decided they did not want to waste such a valuable resource by not keeping her in her leadership role.

3. Reject the request
   An employer can refuse an application if they have a good business reason for doing so. There are eight possible reasons:

   - the burden of additional costs
   - an inability to reorganise work among existing staff
   - an inability to recruit additional staff
   - a detrimental impact on quality
   - a detrimental impact on performance
   - a detrimental effect on ability to meet customer demand
   - insufficient work for the periods the employee proposes to work
   - a planned structural change to your business

If a request is rejected, employees should be allowed an opportunity to appeal the decision. Discussing the decision may reveal new information or modifications which may make the request acceptable or change the balance of pros and cons for the school. It may also highlight any omission in following a reasonable procedure when considering the application which the school will seek to address. As we go to press, the DfE are holding a consultation which would considerably reduce this list. Reasons which remain are likely to be very specific.

Flexible working requests

A request for flexible working should include:

- the date of their application
- the change to working conditions they are seeking
- when they would like the change to come into effect

- what effect, if any, they think the requested change would have on the school and how, in their opinion, any such effect might be dealt with
- a statement that this is a statutory request
- if and when they have made a previous application for flexible working

If an employee fails to attend a meeting to discuss the application, including any appeal, without a good reason, the school can consider the request withdrawn and must inform the employee.

Flexible Teacher Talent advice on making a flexible working request

We support individual teachers and school leaders with their requests for flexible working and over the years we have given advice to many people and supported them with their applications. Some of the advice we give is bespoke to the individual's situation and school context but there are some common themes in our suggestions.

There is no need to emphasise your "why"
The reason that you want to work flexibly is not necessarily part of the consideration for your school. If you do not want to share details of your childcare arrangements or the caring needs that your elderly parent requires then you do not have to. It may be useful to give details if you would not be able to work at certain times, i.e. you want to start after 9am or have Wednesday mornings off site etc. If you are making an application for flexible working due to your disability, then you may be entitled to consideration under the reasonable adjustments requirement of the Equality Act, so some details may be required.

Emphasise the positives
You should focus on the benefits the proposed arrangements will create for both you and the school. Different arrangements will have different advantages, i.e. work from home will allow you to focus undistracted on administrative or strategic tasks, job-share will provide twice the ideas and allow refreshed energy and variety, and so on. This can be hard to do if you are applying at a time when your confidence is low or when you know that the school does not consider flexible working to have a positive impact.

Anticipate their issues
Try and foresee what their issues are likely to be and plan how these could be addressed. If they are likely to raise a question about the weekly team meeting, think about how you might attend remotely or catch up later. If they are worried about timetabling, try and understand how this could be planned to make it work, i.e. can you share certain classes or specialise in certain phases or subjects.

Do not take it personally
If the school rejects your application, it is more often than not because of their concerns about flexible working generally or because they are worried about 'opening the floodgates', not to upset you. We often speak to women returning from maternity leave and making flexible working requests who felt the rejection was a way of forcing them out of their role,

but it is rarely a reflection of how the school values you. In fact, in a contrary way it may actually be a sign of how much they value you: they want to keep you in post full time.

Find role models

Use case studies to show that flexible working can work in your role. These are most effective if they are in context similar to your school. The DfE, the Chartered College of Teaching and Flexible Teacher Talent all have case studies available on their websites. Emma Turner's book *Let's Talk about Flex* also has some good examples of flexible working in schools.

Use support networks

If you cannot find suitable case studies, then reach out to others who may be able to help. Networks such as WomenEd and The MTPT Project, as well as Flexible Teacher Talent, can help to provide role models and to support you with the application process. Furthermore, they may be able to provide support and mentoring or coaching when you begin your flexible role or search for one.

Be flexible

The more flexibility you can offer in terms of days out of school or openness to alternative arrangements the better. After you make the initial application, there should be opportunity to discuss it with someone and there may be ways that you can address their concerns by being flexible about the arrangements that work for you. Be open-minded too – Lindsay originally requested that her 0.6 timetable be on any three consecutive days but the way the timetable worked it could only be offered as Monday, Wednesday, Thursday in school and she came to love that arrangement. It broke up the week, made workload more manageable and allowed her to arrive at school refreshed each day (even if the baby had been up all night).

Flexible working policies

At the Festival of Education in 2018, Lindsay took part in a panel discussion called 'Making Flexible Working Work' with Anna Trethaway. It was standing room only in the session and one audience member was moved to tears by hearing the stories of successful flexible working and to see others sharing their frustration about the difficulties they faced. In her blog about it for TES after the event, Anna wrote about the approach of some senior leaders saying things like 'it's too complicated to implement at scale' and 'we don't do part-time working here' (Trethaway, 2018). There is no legal requirement to offer flexible working to everyone or to grant every request but there is a legal requirement to consider every statutory request which is made on its own merits. In that same blog, Anna describes how many teachers have been 'bruised' by the negotiation process of trying to secure flexible work and how others were leaving the profession due to lack of flexible working and part-time opportunities.

The NAHT supports the adoption of flexible working for teachers and school leaders. It acknowledges that delivering these opportunities may be a complex matter, but encourages school leaders to be committed to facilitating approaches to flexible working that deliver benefits for pupils. Ofsted supports every school's right to decide the best use of their workforce, and nothing in Ofsted's inspection framework should be considered opposition to flexible working. The National Governance Association encourages governing boards to lead the way in the development of progressive employment practices including flexible working that contribute to a healthy working environment and thus to both attracting and retaining high-quality staff.

Having a good, clear, flexible working policy is one way to make it easier for schools to manage and consider flexible working requests and hopefully to allow them to facilitate working arrangements that retain happy, healthy staff in a way that ultimately benefits pupils. Having a flexible working policy is not a legal requirement but adhering to the statutory guidance is required by law so at the very base level, having a good working policy is an effective way to ensure those requirements are met.

Q & A: Danielle Ayres, Employment Law Specialist and Partner at Gorvins Solicitors

What should be included in flexible working policy?

Employers do not need a formal policy and often, may just simply state within any Employee Handbook that they will adhere to statutory provisions should the need arise.

If an organisation wants to have a flexible working policy, I would suggest looking at the ACAS guide that is available, together with the legislation, to make sure that the policy is compliant.

While this is not an exhaustive list, at the very least a policy should include:

1. What flexible working is and perhaps provide some examples of the type of flexible working – reduced days, compressed hours, job-share (see Chapter 4 to consider the types of flexible working which would most suit your context).
2. Who can make a request – an employee must have at least 26 weeks' continuous service to make a request and can only make one flexible working request in any 12-month period.
3. How to submit a flexible working request – who it should be sent to and what it must include.
4. The process that will follow receipt of the request – meeting with the employee, timings and appeal process.
5. A mention of whether trial periods will be offered.
6. What will happen if the request is rejected/accepted.

It is not a 'one size fits all' when it comes to policies, so this needs to be tailored to the work which the organisation carries out and how they do that.

On what basis can a flexible working request be turned down?

There are only eight reasons an employer can turn down a statutory flexible working request, and these are as follows:

- planned structural changes
- the burden of additional costs
- quality or standards will suffer

- they will not be able to recruit additional staff
- performance will suffer
- will not be able to reorganise work among existing staff
- will struggle to meet customer demand
- lack of work during the periods you propose to work

An employer should always try and back up the decision they have made. If there is evidence to support their decision, this should be provided to make the process as transparent as possible and any decision should be fully explained.

What happens if an employee wants to challenge a decision to refuse a flexible working request?

There is no right of appeal against a decision. However, most company policies and employers do offer that right. It is good practice to do so and even where no right of appeal is given, an employee can still write to state their thoughts and comments on the decision itself. This would then need to be dealt with as an appeal.

If an employee is still unhappy after the appeal, or on receipt of a decision where the right to appeal is not given, they can raise a grievance complaint if they feel the procedure has not been followed correctly, or the decision is completely wrong. This is not another 'crack at the whip' of their request though; it is simply to consider whether the process has been done properly. The next step would be to raise a Tribunal claim, which will involve firstly instigating ACAS Early Conciliation. This is a claim that an employee can raise regardless of whether their employment is continuing or coming to an end. It may also include a discrimination claim, depending upon the circumstances and reason for the rejection.

If one flexible working request is granted, will schools have to grant them all?

No, each case should be considered at the time that it is made, on the basis of the employer's circumstances at that time. While it might be ok to accept someone's request at one point, that may not be feasible at a later date. However, where possible an employer should try and find a workable solution and must consider requests in a reasonable manner.

Do schools have to offer flexible working?

An employer cannot say that they do not allow flexible working. To do so may be discriminatory. If an employer receives a request, they must consider it and deal with it in a reasonable manner. It is not enough for them to say that they do not offer flexible working. They have to look at the request that is being presented and properly consider whether that could work, or if not, if any alternatives can be suggested.

Can flexible working requests be agreed on a trial basis?

Yes, it can and it is often beneficial to do so for both parties to see if the flexible working arrangement can indeed work for them both, or if any problems arise. This would be done before permanently implementing an arrangement. The length of the trial period can be agreed between the parties at the outset and reviewed on a regular basis throughout.

One point that should be made here is that a decision in relation to a formal flexible working request should be given within three months of the request being made. This can be extended with agreement between the parties and therefore if there is to be a trial period before the final decision is reached, agreement to extend the statutory time limit should be made in writing.

(Continued)

Can the school and the employee negotiate on the details of the flexible working request and what is the process for this?

Yes, usually this is done as part of the process. The request goes in, and then parties meet to discuss what the employee is proposing. If that cannot be accommodated, then the employer and the employee can discuss alternative arrangements, with both giving their opinion and views on what will work and any problems or issues that they can see arising. Once an arrangement is agreed, the individual's contractual terms will be amended. This is a permanent change to their contract of employment and after that it is extremely difficult to agree any variations, unless both parties are happy to do so.

Can staff on maternity or parental leave be asked to attend meeting to discuss flexible working requests?

Yes, they can, but their situation should always be accommodated. For example, looking at whether the meeting can be done via Zoom or other video link. It can also be done over the telephone. These meetings are often better in person though and therefore, consideration should be given to the fact that the person is on maternity leave or parental leave, so should be set up at a time which suits them or allowances be made. For example, if they are breastfeeding, then they should be allowed to bring the baby with them, or set a time for the meeting when someone else can look after the baby, or make sure it is done around feeding times.

If workers have a health condition or special need do they have any special rights in terms of flexible working requests?

If an employee is classed as disabled under the Equality Act, they should not have to make a flexible working request for adjustments to be made to their working pattern if it is required as a result of their condition. This should be something that is considered by their employer, in any event, as they are under an obligation to ensure that reasonable adjustments are made to ensure that employees with disabilities are not substantially disadvantaged while doing their job. They must allow disabled employees to access the same opportunities, training and services as non-disabled employees. Most employers only think this applies to employees with physical disabilities, but the duty arises for any employee who has a disability, whether that be physical, or mental health conditions.

Adjustments might include 'provisions, criteria and practices' which place disabled employees in a less favourable position, or there may be physical features of the premises in which they work which make it impossible or difficult for them to do their job. With a slight change, or acceptance that something needs to be put in place or changed, then that individual may be able to work without a problem. This could include making changes to the workplace, i.e. installing a ramp for a wheelchair user, or changes to the employee's workstation – lowering/lifting the desk level, or providing specialist equipment to enable that person to do their job effectively. It could also include reducing hours or days of work on a temporary or permanent basis, ensuring that any absence relating to their disability is not recorded in the same way as other general absences.

It may be that the employee makes a formal flexible working request to ask the employer to make these changes, but in those cases, the employer cannot simply turn the request down as a result of one of the eight statutory reasons discussed earlier. They must also consider their duties under the Equality Act and be mindful of a potential disability discrimination claim.

In terms of best practice, there are some other considerations regarding flexible working requests.

A letter or a form?

Some schools provide a proforma or application form for staff to fill in if they are requesting flexible working. Others request a letter and outline what should be included. There may be advantages to a proforma in terms of considering the information provided but also for the purpose of reminding employees what to include/ cover in their application. Examples of proforma can be found online, including one from the London Borough of Tower Hamlets (LBTH, 2018).

Communication while not in school

If the person making an application for flexible working is not currently in school, either because they are on parental leave or for some other reason such as sickness absence, consider how best to communicate with them. Would they prefer to speak on the phone or by e-mail? If by e-mail, on their school or personal account? Are certain times of the day or days of the week best for conversations or meetings and how should they take place? In person, through video conferencing or as a phone call?

Precedent

Just because one request for flexible working is granted does not mean that others in a similar situation also have to be. Each case should be considered on its own particular merits and the balance between any specific costs and benefits will depend on the school's circumstances at that moment in time. However, if a very similar request has previously been granted, the school will have to be clear in justifying why another subsequent one has not been. Similarly, it is not reasonable to say that you will not consider an application because a similar one was turned down in the past – the circumstances may be different in this case at this time.

Governors

How much involvement, if any, governors have in the decision about flexible working will depend on the school's policy. Sometimes the role of the governing body is only to consider applications for flexible working from the headteacher themself, but they could be involved in the appeal process or they could be asked to consider each application, or applications for certain types of role. The aim of a flexible working policy is to allow senior leaders to work with employees to try and identify solutions, where possible, that suit both the individual and the school. Involving governors in this process may help schools to find solutions.

Timetabling

In secondary schools, the timetable is the most frequently given reason for refusing flexibility. If timetablers or primary colleagues in charge of the curriculum are open to flexible working and are involved in decisions about flexible working requests, then they may be able to provide creative and beneficial solutions to accommodate flexible working requests. Upskilling members of staff to give them an understanding of the timetable or curriculum planning process can help them to appreciate the constraints but also allow them to contribute ideas on making flexibility work.

Sharing

How widely available or easy to find is the school's flexible working policy? If it is hard to access, then people may not be able to clearly follow the procedures required. All staff should have access to the policy and all line managers should have an idea of how it works and how to use it. Ideally, line managers will be best placed to have a conversation in advance of a formal application which irons out most of the detail setting any applicant up for success. Sharing it with colleagues who are likely to need it such as those off on parental leave might be a good idea but flexible working requests are not just for parents and carers so it should really be shared more widely. Particularly if decisions regarding timetable or class set ups are required at certain times of the year, schools may wish to encourage staff to apply for flexible working before a certain date so that they can consider as many flexible working requests as possible at one time. Obviously, this is not always possible as needs and circumstances can change and require flexibility at any time of the school year.

Communicating a rejection

If the school have considered an application for flexible working but feel unable to accept it, then they should be mindful of how upsetting that may be for the employee. If the application was made because current circumstances in their life require flexible working, then they may feel or be unable to continue in their role after receiving this rejection. They may feel unvalued or even pushed out. They might feel that the decision was unjust or the process unfair. This can be mitigated if the decision is conveyed with empathy and clarity. Explain why the school was not able to accept the request and the process that they went through when considering it. Offer the chance to apply again in 12-months' time, or even waive that statutory period and offer to consider a further request at a different time when circumstances may have changed, for example, after the May half-term break when new staffing changes or pupil numbers for the following year may have come to light.

Other legal issues

The Equality Act 2010

Schools have specific duties under the Equality Act 2010. As an employer, a school must not discriminate against an existing employee in respect of the benefits, facilities and services it offers to its employees including training opportunities, promotion or dismissal.

Protected characteristics

- Sex
- Race
- Religion or belief
- Sexual orientation
- Gender reassignment
- Pregnancy and maternity
- Age
- Disability

Flexible working requests should not be turned down due to discrimination because someone has one of these protected characteristics. That is unlawful. Indirect discrimination is where a policy or practice, though applied equally to all, has a disproportionate impact on a particular group with a protected characteristic. This may apply to flexible working policies if most or all of the requests are coming from those returning from maternity leave or nearing retirement. Schools cannot discriminate against someone because of something that arises from their disability. Schools must also make reasonable adjustments to arrangements or practices to alleviate disadvantage and this may include altering patterns of work.

Part-time workers (prevention of less favourable treatment) regulations 2000

The law protects part-time workers from being treated less favourably than equivalent full-time workers just because they are part-time. They should get the same treatment for:

- pay rates (including sick pay, maternity, paternity and adoption leave and pay)
- pension opportunities and benefits
- holidays
- training and career development
- selection for promotion and transfer, or for redundancy
- opportunities for career breaks

Some benefits are applied 'pro rata' (in proportion to hours worked). There are also some situations when employers do not have to treat part-time workers in the same way as full-time employees if they are able to show 'objective justification' (a good reason to do so).

If part-time workers feel that they have been treated unfairly, they should first discuss it with their employer or trade union representative. They have the right to request a written statement of the reasons for the treatment and schools have 21 days to respond. If the worker is not satisfied that the reason given was objectively justified, they may be able to take a case to an employment tribunal.

School teachers' pay and conditions document 2020

The DfE set out the statutory requirements for teachers' pay and conditions for maintained schools in England and schools and local authorities (LAs) must abide by these (STPCD, 2020). Academies and free schools do not have to adhere to them but many still use them as their basis for their policies on pay and conditions.

With regard to part-time teachers, it has a number of interesting points:

- The salary and any allowances of a part-time teacher must be determined in accordance with the pro rata principle. This includes any teaching and learning responsibilities (TLR) payments except for TLR3s which should be paid in full.
- Part-time teachers must be available for work for the proportion of 1,265 hours which corresponds to the proportion of their contracted time. E.g. 0.8 contract, 1,012 hours
- Part-time teachers cannot be required to work on any day of the week or part of any day of the week on which they are not normally required to work under their contract (work includes teaching pupils and/or performing other duties).
- Part-time teachers may be required to carry out duties other than teaching pupils outside school sessions on any day on which they normally work (whether the teacher is normally required for a full or part day).
- Part-time teachers cannot be required to work or attend non-pupil days, or parts of days, on days they do not normally work (but they can work by mutual agreement with the headteacher). However, they can be required to undertake work within their allocation of directed time beyond the school's timetabled teaching week.
- Part-time teachers should be provided with a written agreed statement which sets out the expectations of the school, and the part-time teacher, regarding the deployment of working time. Including both timetabled teaching time and leadership and management time. It should also set out the expectations of the school in respect of directed time which is to be deployed beyond the school day.

TLR payments for part-time employees

A Twitter poll by Lindsay in July 2020 showed that 24 per cent of part-time teachers with TLR were paid the full TLR amount for completing the entire role and 26 per cent were paid their TLR pro rata, but were only expected to complete a proportion of the role. In other words, they are paid for the proportion of the work they do. However, 45 per cent of respondents said they were paid only a proportion of the TLR pay but were expected to complete all of the responsibilities. A further 5 per cent had this set up but with some kind of extra incentive such as extra non-contact time or less form time. So, around half of those responding to the survey did their entire leadership role, but for partial pay.

What the STPCD (School Teachers' Pay and Conditions Document) does not make clear when it states that TLR1 and TLR2 payments should be paid pro rata is that the attached responsibilities should also be pro rata otherwise teachers are not being fairly remunerated for their work. Surely this was not the aim of the STPCD guidance as it breeches the Part Time Workers Regulations and possibly The Equality Act too through indirect discrimination.

Why then might this be happening? Maybe schools are trying to follow the STPCD guidelines too closely and missing the bigger picture. Maybe it is too hard to pro rata the responsibilities, i.e. how do you work out what 0.6 of the literacy leader role is? Maybe workers are just so grateful to be able to work flexibly that they accept that they will have to take on unpaid work and responsibility. Maybe it is mostly women who are affected by this and the confidence gap means they are not questioning or negotiating it. Maybe there is just such a lack of transparency in pay arrangements that people do not know it is happening or that it should not be.

It isn't just us who think this is unacceptable. #WomenEd cofounder Dame Vivienne Porritt is very clear in her assertion and belief that if TLR payments are pro rata, then so too should responsibilities be pro rata (Porritt, 2021). Where a leader is part-time they should either have full responsibility for full pay or partial responsibility for partial pay as anything else is certainly unfair and possibly discriminatory and illegal.

A number of parts of the STPCD (2020) relate specifically to discrimination against part-time staff:

- 'To avoid claims of discrimination against part-time teachers, schools should, as a minimum, ensure that their arrangements for the deployment of part-time teachers do not breach the relevant legal provisions regarding equal opportunities and unlawful discrimination.'
- 'The part-time teacher should not have a greater proportion of their directed time allocated outside their normal sessions than is the case for full-time teachers, as this may amount to discrimination.'
- 'The headteacher remains duty bound to have regard to the work-life balance of such staff and should ensure that the workload of part-time members of the leadership group and those on the pay range for leading practitioners is reasonable and that they are treated fairly in comparison with their full-time equivalents.'

This may seem like a great deal of legal and statutory guidance for school leaders to get to grips with but really at the heart of it, it is quite simple: schools should act in a reasonable and non-discriminatory way with regard to flexible working requests and the management of their existing flexible workers. While the current government consultation for flexible working from day one of employment and the right to make multiple requests within twelve months is underway, flexible working requests should be considered fairly, properly and with due care to any disability or the protection of certain characteristics. Part-time teachers and leaders should not be asked to do more than the proportion of the work they are paid for and be given fair expectations, opportunities and support in relation to their work. Headteachers, line managers, school business managers and HR managers all need to know these laws and guidelines and ensure that they act within them.

Summary

This chapter has described:

- How legal and statutory issues might impact flexible working in schools
- What to include in a flexible working policy or flexible working request
- Best practice in terms on flexible working policies in schools

References

ACAS (2014). Code of practice for handling requests in a reasonable manner. Available at: https://www.acas.org.uk/acas-code-of-practice-on-flexible-working-requests/html.

Turner, E. (2020). *Let's Talk About Flex: Flipping the Flexible Working Narrative for Education*. Suffolk: John Catt.

Trethaway, A. (2018). *Flexible Working at School A Quick Guide*. London: TES. Available at: https://www.tes.com/news/flexible-working-school-quick-guide.

LBTH (2018). *Flexible Working – LBTH Model Policy for Schools May 2018.pdf Tower Hamlets Model Policy*. London: LBTH. Available at: https://www.benjonson.towerhamlets.sch.uk/files/policies/personnel/Flexible%20Working%20-%20LBTH%20model%20policy%20for%20schools%20May2018.pdf.

STPCD (2020) *School Teachers' Pay and Conditions Document 2020 and Guidance on School Teachers' Pay and Conditions*. STPCD. Available at: https://www.gov.uk/government/publications/school-teachers-pay-and-conditions; https://assets.publishing.service.gov.uk/government/uploads/system/uploads/attachment_data/file/920904/2020_STPCD_FINAL_230920.pdf.

Patience, L. (2017, 17 October). Tweet. Available at: www.twitter.com/mumsyme. https://twitter.com/Mumsyme/status/920364498275454979 (accessed 14 December 2020).

Patience, L. (2020, 20 July). Tweet. Available at: www.twitter.com/mumsyme. https://twitter.com/Mumsyme/status/1285257278740992002 (accessed 14 December 2020).

Porritt, V (2021, 6 February). Tweet. Available at: www.twitter.com/womened. https://twitter.com/WomenEd/status/1358188963614310402?s=20 (accessed 17 February 2021).

6

FLEXIBLE RECRUITMENT

In this chapter we will:

- Discuss some of the difficulties and benefits of flexible recruitment
- Consider how flexible working can be built into the recruitment process
- Investigate different ways to advertise and apply for roles in school with flexibility

Introduction

Traditional recruitment processes in school can be complex and fraught with difficulty. Termly notice deadlines, changing requirements for option subjects, student numbers not confirmed until late in the summer term, a high proportion of employees in the demographic where parental leave is common, retention issues (particularly with early career teachers), all combine with cost pressures due to government funding changes, evolving curriculum demands and a shortage of new recruits. Recruitment in schools is also very demanding and time consuming for school leaders and support staff. Shortlisting, DBS checks, assessment tasks at interview, including observed lessons all take a great deal of time and take leaders away from their other responsibilities. So, it is absolutely understandable that for school leaders it could seem that adding the option of flexible working to the process is even more of a headache.

Advertising vacancies or recruiting people?

Your people make your school. The experience and outcomes for pupils rely on you having good teachers in your classrooms and effective leaders managing your schools.

If being open to flexible working allows school to recruit more and better teachers and leaders, then it is clear that the inconvenience is worth it. As mentioned in Chapter 2, flexible working can improve your chances of recruiting graduates, women, those with disabilities, older and more experienced teachers, or career changers. It improves the numbers and quality in your recruitment pools providing better shortlists and better appointments. So, if you want to attract, as well as retain the best candidates in your school, then considering flexible working options is a must.

Recruiting with flexibility can also help to make your staffing leaner in terms of costs and more effective in terms of use of staff time. For example, it can allow you to have just enough teaching hours for Computer Science without having to require some teachers teaching maths outside of their specialism in order to fill up their hours. Having a class share in primary school with two teachers where they both work more than 2.5 days may eliminate the need for PPA cover for that class, so while it initially costs more that just employing one teacher, there are cost savings elsewhere and potentially improved consistency and quality of provision. An increase in on-costs from having part-time workers is often cited as a negative of flexible working, but the majority of employment costs are proportional to the full-time equivalence of the staff. There are some costs for schools which might relate to headcount such as certain IT licensing agreements or subscriptions to external services, but many of these have thresholds rather than cost per individual employee in the headcount. For example, payment for a CPD software programme might be one price for a school with 50–99 employees but a higher price for schools with 100–149 employees, so increasing a school's headcount does not necessarily increase its costs.

Having flexible workers also gives organisations more flexibility – it works both ways: with flexibility for the individuals, there is also flexibility for the school's human resource management. Emma Turner, author of *Let's Talk about Flex: Flipping the flexible working narrative for education*, describes this as 'elasticity' (Turner, 2020) for the organisation. It can help the school be more responsive to changing demand and requirements. For example, if you can reduce or increase the full-time equivalence of your staff body by reducing some members of staff to 0.6 and increasing others to 0.8, this can help school leaders to manage changes in staffing requirements. Some of the reasons this may be required or helpful could include changes to SEN requirements of students or variability in option choices in Key Stages 4 and 5 resulting in more or less demand for certain academic courses. Having staff who want to, or are willing to work flexibly, can help schools to ride the waves of these changes. It means you can have just the right staff hours for the requirements of your pupils, their support and the curriculum. This increased responsiveness allows schools to use staff time effectively so that teachers are able to continue specialising in the subjects, phases and areas they are trained in. This keeps them happy and their workload manageable, but it also means the students in your school get specialist provision which is likely to be of higher quality.

Another benefit of this flexibility for the school is that it allows leaders to be 'lean' in their timetabling and staff deployment. In secondary schools, this allows you to timetable without too much spare capacity in terms of staff teaching loads. It makes it unlikely that you will have to over-recruit and add a full-time teacher to cover just a few hours of timetabled lessons. It also works the other way around. In a particular academic year, there might be lots of additional students choosing A Level Biology. Rather than squeezing too many into one class or pushing current teachers to the maximum, or over their teaching loads, you can recruit a specialist to teach those extra few hours. Alternatively, use the 'give' or flexibility from current flexible workers to increase the provision within the department. So, if you needed an extra 0.2 full-time equivalent hours, you can ask two members of staff who are currently working 0.5 if they would be willing to go up to 0.6 for the year to cover the change in demand.

Timewise report that candidates who need flexibility worry about applying for roles that do not specifically mention it (Timewise, 2019). This results in excellent candidates feeling stuck in their current flexible jobs. They stay at their current school even if it means they neglect career progression in order to retain the flexibility. Schools may be disregarding excellent candidates because they do not apply for vacancies due to the risk of not being able to secure the working pattern they need.

Job design and creation

These practical examples give a flavour of the very specific scenarios which have been successfully used in schools to help retain effective individual teachers. Rather than worrying about the minutiae of logistics and what ifs as a reaction to individuals' requests, school leaders can look at staffing more holistically. Rather than piecing together a puzzle for individuals to fit around the norm of full-time equivalents (FTEs), why not take it back to the vision and values of the school and design jobs that way? A 'goals rather than roles' approach. Many successful organisations outside of education with large HR departments take this approach.

Our service users are our pupils and having high-quality staff in front of them for the requisite number of hours is paramount. Having enough staff to fulfil legal obligations like registration and safeguarding is also crucial. However, we could spend more time thinking creatively about all the other things that teachers and leaders do in our schools. There is much value to be gained from looking at that time when they are not in the classroom. How is that time spent and is it effective in achieving the school priorities? Starting with the priorities for the school, leaders consider not simply who needs to be taught what and when, but also what else needs doing, who can do it and when. So far, so obvious, and we see schools following traditional models with roles like Heads of Year, Subject Leads, Assistant Headteachers with responsibilities for attainment at various Key Stages and so on. The most effective line managers should be confident in understanding how the roles within their team could be shared out or allocated in the most productive and successful way. If we know what our vision is, precisely what jobs need doing and then match those to the skillset of our staff, we can ensure a better fit for the team, get better results and identify any skill gaps in the team. This type of skills audit allows more effective planning for both recruitment and staff training.

Advertising with flexibility

When advertising posts with a view to flexible working, there are a number of different options for schools:

- Advertise a full-time post, but mention being open to flexible working
- Advertise a part-time post with a certain pro rata requirement or range of pro rata arrangements
- Advertise fully flexible roles
- Advertise for people, not roles
- Advertise with flexible options specific to the role

If you offer a vacancy full-time and an applicant asks about flexibility, it can be seen as an annoyance, but try to be open minded about how it could possibly work in your school and in that post. Candidates may raise the question of flexible working before they apply, in informal conversations or during school visits. They might ask about it as part of the interview process, or they may wait until they are offered the post to ask if there could be any consideration of flexible working. Best practice advice from HR specialists outside of the education sector is to wait until you are appointed to a post before you negotiate flexible working. This is to stop discrimination about the desire for flexible working from influencing the recruitment decision. If you are selected as the best person for a role, then an organisation should at least try to accommodate your request for flexibility. The issue with this approach is that if the school cannot provide the arrangements you need, then everyone feels disheartened and the job will have to go to a less qualified or suited applicant who can work full-time. In an ideal world, once you have decided that someone is the best candidate for a role, you should treat them as if they are already a member of staff and afford them the same flexibility. The Chartered Institute of Personnel and Development (CIPD)'s 'Flex from First' campaign calls on organisations and government to make the right to request flexible working a day-one right. At present, in England, Wales and Scotland, the law states that employees can only request flexible working after 26 weeks of employment, with a limit of one request per year (ACAS, 2021). However, this is currently the subject of a DfE consultation and the recommendation is likely to be taken up so that employees no longer need to 'earn' the right to apply for flexibility.

An alternative for schools is to mention flexibility right from the outset of the recruitment process. This can be done by specifying a certain type of flexibility in the job advert such as specifying 0.6 FTE or the role being as a talent partnership (job-share). Additionally, it could be mentioned that staff can take their PPA or non-contact time off-site or that staff receive a certain number of paid leave days or mental health days a year in the information about the school. Sometimes, the mention of flexible working can be more open ended than a specific offer. The advert might just say that the school are open to discussing flexible working or state that they will consider flexible arrangements.

We are increasingly seeing wording that justifies the school's position on flexible working such as explaining the benefits for staff wellbeing. Some explain that the school wants the best people and acknowledges that they might not be available full-time or that they might be in a talent partnership (job-share). Others emphasise the autonomy for staff in choosing a working pattern that works for both the individual and the school. What is important here is that these comments in job adverts and application packs are not just there to tick some diversity or 'good employer' checklist. If schools are encouraging applicants seeking flexible working to apply, then they should have a genuine desire and commitment to making that flexibility both available and successful.

Some examples of wording from job adverts

Contract type: Part Time Pro rata (0.80 FTE).

We would consider 0.4–0.8 FTE for this post.

We are happy to talk about flexible working.

Reasons to join us

- Family-friendly and flexible working policies
- Two days per year paid staff leave days during term time
- PPA time can be taken off-site

The role is based on the school site but with flexible working arrangements, including home working.

Teaching position – Temporary Job-share for 2021 school year: English Teacher – 0.4 FTE

It is envisaged that the standard hours of work will be 8.30 am to 3.00 pm (with a 30-minute unpaid lunch break), Monday to Friday, but we are very open to flexible working requests, and applicants are advised that there will be the opportunity for portions of the work to be completed at home.

We are happy to talk flexible working and offer flexible working for most roles in the organisation, meaning that many of our employees enjoy the freedom of choosing a working pattern that suits them as much as it suits the organisation.

The role is available part-time, job-share or full time. This is because we want the best people for our roles, and we recognise that sometimes those people are not available full time.

We welcome applications from all sections of the community and those interested in job sharing.

(Continued)

This is a full-time, permanent position; however, we would consider a job-share for two candidates looking for a part time.

An organisation called Working Families have a 'Happy to Talk Flexible Working' logo which schools can add to their vacancies page if they are advertising jobs with flexible working options (Working Families, 2021).

It would be remiss to talk about flexible working and recruitment and not mention, again, the work that Headteacher Sue Plant did when she was setting up the John Taylor Free School in September 2018. With a clean slate on staffing for her brand-new school, Sue advertised for and interviewed people rather than filling specified vacancies. Specific roles were not advertised, but all subjects were advertised with the flexibility emphasised and titles were created once Sue had met and interviewed the candidates. There was a wide field of candidates to choose from with 160 applicants for those eleven jobs. In an area where other headteachers were struggling to recruit, she was able to fully staff the school and spent £0 on recruitment. Sue said there was no resistance from the MAT or the governors because if you are attracting high-quality people with the right values, who can argue with getting the right people on the team? Admittedly this was a very specific situation where a school was brand new, but Sue says, "While there is a certain freedom in setting a school up from scratch, we must encourage people in existing schools to be more creative about possibilities".

The rest of the recruitment process

Whether posts are advertised with flexibility or not, there are various points in the rest of the recruitment process when the question of flexible working may arise.

Questions about flexibility may be asked by candidates before they apply, during the interview or assessment process, or after they are offered the role. Any staff who are involved in the process, from the Head to the school receptionist or HR assistant, should be aware of the school's position on flexible working. It is not necessary to have the answers straight away. Good flexible working arrangements are often borne out of compromise and adapting to the needs of the individual and the school. It will rarely be possible to make decisions or answer specific questions on the spot, but leaders can reflect on the needs of individuals and look at how that can work for the school.

Outside of education, organisations put a lot of work into job design and human resource management. They are often dynamic and important strategies for leaders, and a source of competitive advantage. There is a tendency in schools not to look at recruitment and workforce planning in this way. Schools often just do what has always been done in relation to issues of HR. This attitude is holding us back from becoming better, twenty-first century workplaces which get the best out of our people. Our driver is not profit; it is pupil outcomes. For most, our source of funding is public money so resource productivity is arguably more important, not less. Yet we often fail to manage human resources well.

Granted, most school leaders do not have much, if any, experience of job design, flexible working or HR management. In some schools, there are not specialist HR managers or Trust leads to support headteachers with this area. Nevertheless, openness, reflection and innovation can have a hugely positive impact on effective management of HR processes.

Talent partnership (job-shares)

There are a number of different ways that talent partnership (job-sharing) arrangements might be presented in the recruitment process. Some people apply as a talent partnership – they already work together or want to work together. In some recruitment processes, they may be considered and interviewed together as a whole. In other cases, they may apply as individuals and are only appointed if they are identified as the top two candidates. For a candidate who has applied without a partner, there obviously then needs to be a further process for identifying who will do the rest of the role (unless the role can be redesigned to be part-time or the team reorganised in a way that allows part-time). It may be that the second best candidate for the role, internal or external, also wants to work flexibly and they can be set up as a talent partnership. An alternative is that a new recruitment process may have to take place to appoint a talent partner. The probability of this scenario is reduced by mentioning flexibility in the advert in the first instance. If a candidate applied for a full-time position and does not mention job-sharing until they are offered the role, then it can be much harder to find a partner because others who might have applied if the job had been offered with flexibility will not have applied.

Contracts

HR and legal specialists should be consulted on contract design and wording. Some contracts include specific days and hours of working, while some include just FTE proportions. Talent partnership (job-sharing) contracts may be different again depending on the balance of the work and responsibility, and how accountability is distributed. Some schools and trusts have flexibility around working hours and time on site specified in the contracts, i.e. they might say that each year the hours will be reviewed, but will be between 0.5 and 0.6 FTE. Alternatively, they may specify working days or, alternatively, the school may outline that working days and times will be specified each academic year and are subject to change. Expectations around attendance to INSET or hours required on site on a working day may also be specified in the contract. Other aspects of flexibility may not be included in contracts, but just part of other polices, i.e. mental health days or PPA off-site.

Offers and negotiation

If a candidate who has been offered a role raises the issue of flexible working, schools are not currently required to treat it in the same way as they would a formal statutory application for flexible working from an employee who has been employed for more than 26 weeks. Flexibility is essentially part of the negotiation on the terms and pay for the role. Traditionally, the education sector is not big on this type of negotiation and neither heads nor senior leaders will have much experience of dealing with it. What is crucial is to listen to and understand what the individual is asking for, then take that information away and look at what can work for the school. Negotiation should be a process: it should not be a question which is responded to with a yes or a no. We worked with someone recently who applied for a deputy headteacher role, and when offered the job asked if she could do it 0.8 FTE four days a week. The school went away to think about it and came back to her with an offer of 0.9 FTE which could be one nonschool day every other week or one nonschool afternoon a week. She accepted the post on 0.9 FTE and the responsibilities of the role were revised to reflect this 0.1 reduction in pay.

Finding a flexible role

For individuals looking for a new role that is flexible, there are various options. Those looking for flexible working might be coming from a role where they already have flexibility or be seeking a new role because they want flexibility they cannot get in their current role. They may be interested in flexibility because they need it or because they just fancy it: both should be accepted as valid. They may be new to the profession or experienced teachers, they might be changing careers or returning after a break from teaching. There is no particular type of person who will be looking for a flexible role, but there is a chance that those applicants are facing circumstances or changes in their lives that may put them in a particularly vulnerable or sensitive position. Searching for a job or a promotion can be a brutal process and many people find it even more difficult to find a flexible role, but there are ways to secure one.

Search for roles advertised with flexibility

There has been great progress in terms of the number of roles now offered with flexible working. Search functions often allow you to filter for part-time roles but there are also roles advertised as full time, but with wording in the text of the advert about flexible working. Sadly, for some roles, and in some places, there are still very few opportunities offered with flexible working arrangements. Do not give up. There are other ways to find a flexible role – see the following options:

Apply for full-time roles, then approach the question of flexibility

The big question here is whether to mention flexibility before you apply, during the application process or after you are offered the role. If you make enquiries about whether it would be possible to do the role flexibly before you apply, then you save yourself, and the school, from wasting time if it is inflexible. If you mention flexibility on your application form or during any interviews, then it gives the school a chance to consider it before they offer you the role, but if the answer is no, then you have wasted time with the application. Advice from experts outside of the sector is actually to apply for full-time positions and then attempt to negotiate flexibility only if you are offered the role. This removes the prospect of discrimination on the basis of your desire for flexibility and means that if you are the best candidate for the role, then you will be offered it. However, many people feel uncomfortable with this approach for a couple of reasons. The first being that if you get to the stage of being offered a role and then your required flexibility cannot be accommodated, then you have wasted a significant amount of time and effort on the application process. The second concern is about how the school would react to finding out that the candidate they wanted to appoint is not available full time. The risk when applying for a full-time role with no flexibility advertised is that if you are appointed, the school may not be willing or able to accommodate the flexibility you require. There is also a question over how well supported you will be in that school working flexibly if they do grant flexibility post-application. Schools who offer you a role knowing all about your flexible working needs are obviously more likely to be in a position to make your role work flexibly. It comes down really to a decision about how much of a trailblazer you are willing to be. For schools who are unwilling to consider flexible working, making adjustments for a candidate they really want to have working with them might be the only way to start them on the journey to offering flexibility, but this can be difficult for the individual. It requires confidence and courage.

Speculative or general applications

We have seen more and more success recently with speculative applications which are not a traditional way to find roles in the education sector. Teaching roles require certain safer recruitment processes which mean that you should not be able to apply for roles just with submitted CVs, however speculative applications can still work, just slightly differently to how they might in commercial sectors. The idea is that applicants send a CV and covering letter, or just a letter, to schools that they might be interested in working at. The potential applicant shares details about themselves and their experience, but also about what they are looking for in terms of roles, including any flexible working requirements. The school would then keep the details of that person on file and if a vacancy arises which they might be suitable for, then they could be invited to apply. For example, if someone had recently relocated, then they might send a letter to local schools explaining that they were an experienced teacher of humanities and were looking for a role that was four days a week. If a maternity cover position for a Head of Geography role then came up the next term, the school might consider inviting that candidate to apply to cover the teaching part of the role while the Head of Humanities took over the leadership aspects. Another example might be someone writing to a primary school asking to be considered for any part-time Key Stage 1 teaching roles that come up and then, at a later date, a current member of staff wants a talent partnership (job-share) and they would be logistically ideal talent partners. More detail on successful talent partnerships is in Chapter 7. Obviously, this is highly reliant on timing and luck, yet it might be the perfect way for both the individuals and the school to recruit if the timing works out. Some schools are now asking for general applications on the vacancies section of their websites.

Agencies and networks

If you are searching for a new role with some flexibility, it can be an option to use your networks. Organisations such as Flexible Teacher Talent and The Maternity Teacher Paternity Teacher Project will happily post in their social media accounts to see if there is anyone available to job-share or any flexible vacancies coming up. There are also some great vacancy threads like #EduJobs and #teachingvacancyuk on Twitter and networks such as Teach First and We Are In Beta publish weekly vacancy bulletins on social media.

Flexible recruitment is the future

Recruitment in schools can be difficult and time consuming, but it is absolutely crucial to get it right. Outside of the education sector, organisations are using flexible recruitment offers to attract the best candidates and to get the most out of their workforce. CIPD found that 87 per cent of employees would like to work more flexibly, and there is a strong demand from both men and women and across all age ranges (CIPD, 2019). However, 89 per cent of jobs are still not advertised as flexible. If we want schools to be modern and diverse workplaces that are attractive to excellent teachers from a range of backgrounds, then we must get better at flexible recruitment.

Summary

This chapter has described:

- Why flexible working is an important aspect of the complex and important process of recruitment in schools
- How schools can advertise and recruit with flexible working in mind
- The options available to individuals looking for roles with flexible working arrangements in schools

References

ACAS (2021). Accessed at: https://www.acas.org.uk/flexible-working on 25/5/21.
CIPD (2019). Accessed at: https://www.cipd.co.uk/Images/flexible-working-guide-2019-v2_tcm18-58713.pdf on 10/5/21.
Timewise (2019). Accessed at: https://timewise.co.uk/wp-content/uploads/2019/06/Flexible_working_Talent_Imperative.pdf on 10/5/21.
Turner, E. (2020). *Let's Talk About Flex: Flipping the Flexible Working Narrative for Education*. Melton: John Catt Educational.
Working Families (2021). Accessed at: https://workingfamilies.org.uk/employers/httfw/on 10/5/21.

7

TALENT PARTNERSHIPS (JOB-SHARING) IN SCHOOLS

In this chapter we will:

- Explore the various forms talent partnerships can take in schools
- Describe best practice and considerations which will help to make talent partnerships successful
- Discuss ways to address some of the common challenges to talent partnerships in schools

Introduction

Formal job-sharing in teaching is less common than standard part-time arrangements but is gaining popularity. To some extent, many people working part-time as a teacher or school leader could be said to be job-sharing – after all, who teaches the class the rest of the week? Who completes the other administrative or leadership responsibilities? There is an argument that for many working part-time there is a job-sharer doing other parts of the role. Wherever there is a shared group or 'split-class' in a secondary school or PPA cover in a primary school, there is an element of job-sharing, and in the relationships between LSAs and TAs with class teachers. But formal job-sharing is more than that. The definition is 'an arrangement in which two people share the work and pay of a single full-time job' (Lexico Dictionaries), but a genuine job-share is about shared responsibility, shared accountability, shared ideas and shared expertise; a talent partnership.

Talent partnerships in education

Job-sharing in the education sector, as in any sector, can take a variety of forms. Job-shares are usually between two (or more) part-time staff, but they do not have to be. There may be three or four people sharing a role, or the job-sharers might be full time, or the two roles might add up to more than one full-time post.

All of the following examples are talent partnerships in the education sector:

- A Year 5 class taught by two teachers, one who works 3 days and one who works 2 days.
- A co-headship with each co-head working 3 days a week with 0.5 day crossover time.
- Two part-time assistant heads who work 2.5 days each.
- MAT CEOs where two people work full time but share the role.
- Head and Deputy salary combined and split between two full-time post holders who are both coheads.
- SENDCO role and TLR shared between three staff members 2-2-1 days.

Job-sharing arrangements can offer flexibility to employees by allowing them to work flexibly or part-time. Different set-ups will offer different benefits to the individuals involved and to the organisations in which they work, but there are some general benefits of talent partnerships which can be applied across most scenarios.

Benefits of talent partnerships

There are many different aspects of working in a talent partnership which can benefit both the individuals involved and the school. What these benefits are depends on those involved and the specific context but there are benefits to decision-making, sharing workload, accountability, productivity, confidence, specialisation, retention and succession planning.

Two heads are better than one

Having the thoughts, contribution, ideas and problem-solving skills of two teachers for the price of one has obvious benefits. Also, for the children, being able to spend time and work with two different people may have positive benefits. A change in style can add variety and give different children a chance to excel or to form a strong bond with the teachers. They may have varying specialisms or areas of expertise, allowing the children to have expert tuition and meaning that teachers can specialise rather than teaching outside of their strengths or experience. In the early years of primary school, having more than one teacher might replicate the nursery or other early years setting experience that many children have had and ease transition. Similarly, having different teachers in Year 5 or Year 6 is good preparation for the move into secondary school. It follows that consideration of how many adults pupils interact with is crucial when planning shared classes at secondary. If children who go into Year 7 are already overwhelmed by having so many different teachers, then having more than one science or English teacher may exacerbate the problem. This does not mean that classes cannot be split at secondary, only that consideration needs to be given as to where the sharing takes place. There is an argument that having people who are jointly responsible for a role may create additional accountability as they feel additional responsibility to do well for the job-share partner and there is a great deal more close monitoring and understanding of the tasks at hand.

> *Well, if you are a parent, answer this question: who would you prefer your child to be taught by – one pedestrian full-time teacher or two sparkling part-time teachers on a job share? The answer will always be the latter, obviously.*
>
> John Tompsett, Headteacher, Huntington School (Tomsett, 2020)

Energy levels

Being a teacher can be really hard work. It is often exhausting, physically demanding, emotionally draining and the profession continues to report high workload (TUC, 2019) and stress levels (Renn, 2020). If a teacher only works one half or part of the week, it is much easier to maintain energy levels and enthusiasm for those days than it would be for five full days. This may be particularly true for those with health issues, or pregnant or menopausal women, or those nearing retirement. There is an argument that newly qualified teachers would benefit from reduced timetables for more than their first year to help to prevent burnout and try to retain some of those early career teachers who leave in their first five years of teaching. Think how wonderful it might be for the children to get a new teacher mid-week who is refreshed, enthusiastic and ready to work. This is certainly not a solution to workload issues in the profession and the job should not be one that cannot be done full time because it is so exhausting and overwhelming – there are key changes that need to take place to address this separately. One of the key barriers identified in the DfE's Recruitment and Retention Strategy is that 'The wider context in which headteachers operate can create pressure that leads to excessive workload that distracts teachers from teaching'. However, there are times in people's lives when their energy levels would be improved if they were not working full time. If we cannot adapt to that and adopt a way of working that supports it, then we will lose those people from our schools, probably forever.

Retention of expertise and succession planning

Following on from the previous point, there are times in people's lives where they may want or need to work flexibly and if they cannot, then they will either leave the school or profession, or they will be unhappy and struggle with working full time. Being able to keep these staff in our schools is so important for the students. If someone is a valued teacher or school leader, it is surely better to have them for some of the time rather than not at all.

In terms of succession planning, it can be helpful, if one job-share partner is new, to learn from a more established one or, when there is a vacancy for the supply teacher or temporary appointment, to have the support of someone who already knows what is going on and how the job works. This has benefits for the children too; rather than having a completely new teacher to get used to, they will still have the consistency of one of their original teachers while they acclimatise to the new arrangement.

Job-sharing can also be a great way to give people confidence to step up to leadership positions. For women in particular, there are well-documented studies showing a lack of confidence when applying for promotions or new jobs. Research has shown that women only apply for roles if they think they meet 100 per cent of the criteria listed. Men apply if they think they meet 60 per cent of the requirements (Sandberg, 2013). They are more likely to feel unqualified and not ready to step up, and impostor syndrome can be a real barrier. Zenger Folkman's research shows that women's confidence increases over their lives but in their mid-20s, women were ranked in the 32nd percentile for confidence while men were in the 49th percentile (Folkman, 2021). If a teacher did not feel confident to apply for a full-time Head of Department role, but was given the opportunity to apply as part of a talent partnership with another, more experienced colleague, then they might be more willing to give it a try and learn on the job with support. This could be a good way to address the gender imbalance in school leadership and help to train and prepare new generations of school leaders who are well prepared to face the challenges of the job.

Specialisation and expertise

As an economics teacher, for many years now Lindsay has only taught the macroeconomics units on the A Level course. As an examiner for the macroeconomics paper, she knows the content inside out and understands the types of questions that might be asked and how the answers are assessed. Her topical knowledge and examples are up to date and detailed. Her lesson planning is easier because she has taught the content so many times before – usually to more than one class per year – allowing reflections and refinement each time. This reduces workload, makes her more confident in her teaching and gives her students much better expert delivery than if she was trying to teach all aspects of the specification. There are often grumbles about the issues with having 'split-classes', but having two teachers at A Level specialising in different parts of the course works really well for a subject like Economics and for the teaching and workload in the department.

The benefits of specialisation can apply in many different scenarios:

- Primary teachers focusing on phonics or maths, science or languages, PE or music
- Science teachers focusing on one particular discipline rather than teaching across the whole double or triple science specification
- Geography teachers specialising in human or physical geography
- History teachers using their expertise in different themes, topics or eras
- Teachers working on different skills or aspects of development
- Senior leaders sharing responsibilities based on their strengths, for example, one delivering presentation and another crunching the data
- Heads of Department specialising in their areas of expertise such as one working on Key Stage 4 and the other Key Stage 5

Good teachers should be able to teach well across the required phase or exam and repeating content will hone and refine that teacher's specialism. We can use flexibility to improve and perfect one area of our subject knowledge, without losing the skills to teach another. In the macroeconomics example, Lindsay is still able to support her students with questions about and links to microeconomics in synoptic topics. In the co-headship model from chapter 3, Lynn Williams explains that, "Over time our areas of specialism took shape and indeed began to polarise as each gained expertise in areas of particular interest, by following our passions through CPD and other external work. My co-head partner had a role delivering leadership training through the national college on her 'days off'. I became a data specialist and invested time learning about effective data management tools." In both of these examples, there is an expectation of being able to adequately fulfill the whole role while being able to develop an expertise and specialism in part of the role. Talent partnerships develop specialist expertise in a way a full-time role may not allow.

The qualities of effective talent partners (job-shares)

There are some skills and qualities that are likely to make job-sharers more effective:

- High level of job motivation/ proactive/ always always takes the initiative
- Flexibility, adaptability and willing attitude
- Self-assured and self-aware
- Organised, strong project management skills, good eye for detail
- Well disciplined/ability to focus
- Drive for results, high achievement and continuous improvement focused
- Good communicator/strong interpersonal skills and conflict resolution capability
- Strong decision-making and sound judgement
- Takes full ownership and responsibility
- Trustworthy and trusting
- Collaborative working style, strong team player, a solver, not a blamer

These are all skills an employer wants to see in the majority of their workforce. In a genuine partnership, 'my' success becomes 'our' success, just as problems require 'our' solutions and 'we' are responsible for mistakes. That is a mature attitude, to take responsibility publicly for something which someone else allowed, knowing that they would mirror our actions if the situation were reversed. This kind of attitude and approach would benefit colleagues at all levels of the school, whether they were in partnerships or not. These skills and qualities, and the embracing of shared accountability and collaborative problem solving, would lead to much happier, healthier organisations where better decisions were made and staff felt a strong sense of community, loyalty and drive to improve.

Advice on sharing classes

An increase in flexible working opportunities inevitably means more teachers sharing classes. At primary level, this might be more job-shares or increased use of subject specialists taking part of the curriculum, meaning the main class teacher has more time away from the class. At secondary level, it means more 'split classes' where classes are taught by more than one member of staff, e.g. a Year 9 English class may have three hours a week with one teacher and two hours a week with another. Despite a lack of evidence, sharing classes like this is often seen negatively. There are plenty of ways of making class sharing more effective and avoiding some of the anticipated potential issues.

Whether you are sharing a job, or simply sharing a class, valuable preparation time will ensure that the partnership works. Even if you are not working flexibly at the moment, this is valuable self-development and can help you analyse your own strengths.

Shared responsibility for the learning of a group of pupils has many advantages, but these are at risk of being lost if we do not prepare adequately for the change. Have a go at following these simple steps:

1. Recognise our own biases, preconceptions, limitations and strengths.
2. Decide on the most effective methods of communication.
3. Organise the logistics of curriculum delivery.

Recognising bias, preconceptions and strengths

We are human. We hold biases and preconceptions which might be based on past experiences or on very little evidence, a gut feeling. These are only damaging when we do not recognise and understand them.

To CEOs with shared responsibility, organisation Capability Jane gives the following advice on how to appear in front of their service users and workforce:

> *Loyalty and a united front as a partnership are critical. The team will identify any chinks and this could undermine the partnership.*
>
> (Capability Jane, 2011)

Their research shows that job-shares in any sector fail when the impression is that the share was imposed – not chosen – and where there is a mismatch in capabilities or motivation. Anyone who has worked with them will know that children will pick up unconscious cues from a teacher very quickly.

When sharing a class, it is common to have thoughts which highlight either our bias about someone else, our own limitations or both. We might believe that the other teacher is less experienced, or that they will have better subject knowledge than us, or that our life would be simpler if we taught the class all on our own. Acknowledging these thoughts and biases means we can focus on the strengths that we each bring to the partnership.

Children in our care will make the most progress when we start to see differences of teaching style, working pattern or level of experience as a strength. When we recognise that the best teachers are also learners, then we can start to see shared responsibility as an advantage and an opportunity.

Preparation

Great partnerships rely on the people who make them. Self-awareness is crucial to success, so examine your suitability for the role. Take time to reflect honestly and actually write down in your journal the answers to the following questions:

- Do you have a focused approach to your work? Are you proactive? Are you well-disciplined and able to focus? Are you a solver, not a blamer? Are you a good communicator? Are you naturally collaborative? Organised? Adaptable? Trusting? Are you happy to share success? Take ownership and responsibility?
- Are you aware of your first impressions and preconceptions of the person you will share the class with?
- Have you considered how they might be feeling about sharing a class with you?
- What are the strengths and the value you will add to the partnership?
- What is it that you think will learn from the partnership?
- On a whole school level, have you considered which classes are never shared and why? For example, why are Year 11 who know the school and teachers 'protected' from shared classes while Year 7 who come from primary with one or two teachers are often 'split' across faculties? Is this about 'protection' or accountability?

Communication

Sharing a class demands regular and positive conversations. These are critical to our teaching practice and relate to the following DfE Teacher Standards:

- Know when and how to differentiate appropriately, using approaches which enable pupils to be taught effectively
- Have a secure understanding of how a range of factors can inhibit pupils' ability to learn, and how best to overcome these
- Demonstrate an awareness of the physical, social and intellectual development of children, and know how to adapt teaching to support pupils' education at different stages of development

- Demonstrate knowledge and understanding of how pupils learn and how this impacts on teaching

Once teachers complete the NQT year, time is rarely allocated for regular communication with another invested adult about the learning, progress and achievement of pupils within a specific class. Frequent sharing of successes, reflecting on our individual practice and articulating this to someone else succinctly is immensely empowering for us and for our pupils.

Communication tips

- Allow for time each week to discuss progress and medium-term planning. Be flexible about this at the start as there will be more to feedback. Investment at the beginning of the partnership will pay dividends later in the academic year.
- Agree on a shared seating plan and update each other with any changes and reasons for these.
- Agree on routines for homework – both allocation and collection.
- Communicate updates on achievement and behaviour and, where appropriate, advice regarding activities that can follow the previous learning. If this information is sent via e-mail, it does not need to be acknowledged in writing by your talent partner; simply acted upon and responded to later once their lesson has been taught.
- Where possible, drop in to lessons taken by your teaching partner. Take an interest in what the pupils are doing and praise good work where you see it.
- Share the results of this communication with your class. Knowing they are being discussed can mean the world to pupils and hearing authentic feedback from your professional conversations can boost their confidence immeasurably.
- At the start of the year, sit down and work out how you will most equitably share assessment marking, parents' evenings and any other commitments.

Curriculum delivery: semantics matter

- Consider the wording you use to describe the arrangement. Splitting a class and sharing a class are different things entirely and have different implications.
- The curriculum delivered to a Year 12 geography A Level class might be easily split between two teachers and play to each teacher's respective expertise in physical and human geography, whereas a Key Stage 3 english class will require more of a shared approach.
- Initially, it may appear that there is an obvious demarcation in the knowledge and skills which the children need to learn and that splitting the class might work. An english class could in theory be split between english literature and grammar. However, a double lesson of grammar on a Wednesday afternoon might not be something that your class is able to process. That kind of demarcation from splitting can quickly become a disadvantage.
- Whatever you decide, keep reflecting, refining and communicating. You are a powerful partnership of talent bringing two lots of individual expertise to a collaborative role.

Factors to consider when offering talent partnerships

School leaders may see talent partnerships as logistically difficult or impossible in their schools, but there are a growing number of examples of it working successfully across all school contexts and job roles. However, it may not be straightforward to set talent partnerships up in schools and there are some factors which may need to be considered in order for it to run smoothly.

Crossover time

Is it needed? How will it be funded? At primary especially there will need to be shared time to co-ordinate planning and delivery and to discuss the progress and needs of the children. This may mean shared protected time which may be difficult to arrange, but it should also be considered that if co-ordination with their talent partner takes up all of a teacher's allocated PPA time, then they will have to spend additional time doing their own planning and marking. So for talent partnerships to work properly, there should really be additional paid time on both teachers' timetables.

Job design

How will roles and responsibilities be shared or split? Talent partnerships are actually quite different to what Dr Charlotte Gascoigne of Timewise referred to at the 2018 Festival of Education as a job split rather than a job-share (Gascoigne and Kelliher, 2017). The latter is more like one role done seamlessly between two people, whereas the former is two separate people each doing a specific part of the role. Traditionally, job design is not something which schools consider or invest much time in. It is often formed of tradition and convenience rather than strategically and professionally managed as a human resources activity. We follow patterns of working which we have seen as successful, and we tend towards replicating these. We timetable and allocate using traditional roles which have been packaged up over time. A head of subject or head of year is a convenient way to allocate accountability. With a talent partnership, an organisation has two qualified people in post and can therefore be more creative about how the role is adapted and shared. There is an unusual element of freedom where two people are well qualified for a role to become more than the sum of their parts.

> *'The subject leaders and I look at the splits we make. It's not just arbitrary. I have also trained subject leaders over the years; we are in a position now where most of the established subject leaders know the consequences of a split and who best to split classes between.' Mike Bruce, assistant head with responsibility for staffing and curriculum planning – Huntington School when discussing timetabling part time staff.*
>
> (Tomsett, 2020)

Cost

There are additional on-costs of having two employees in place of one. Plus, on top of that, there may be a requirement to cover the cost of having to pay for extra PPA or handover time. Having more than one person in a post may mean that there is more chance of having to recruit again if a job-share partner leaves. However, there will also be potential cost savings in terms of retention of experienced, effective staff rather than recruiting and training new colleagues. Also, in terms of value, there will be benefits that outweigh any cost increases such as the dedication and time put in by the individual partners, the chances of improved recruitment fields, better and cheaper arrangements for cover, and progress made by children.

Compatibility

What is the fit between the talent partners like? If the set-up of the job-share was reactive or done as a last resort, then it is purely down to chance whether the partners will work well together in the role. Strategic management and proactive planning of talent partnerships can help to maximise the chances of success and deploy talent more effectively in the school.

Case study 7.1 Brenzett Primary School

Cassie Young, Head of School and SENDCO at Brenzett Primary School in Kent, suggests either trying to appoint job-share partners who have a very similar way of working, to ensure that pupils are either getting a very similar pedagogic experience whichever person is teaching them, or having partners with diverse curriculum strengths so that the children have the best teacher in front of them for different subjects.

She also provides some other really useful advice for job-sharing in primary settings. She talks about the importance of handover time to discuss plans and individual pupils in directed time together. Particularly in EYFS and Key Stage 1 classes, it may be important to have support staff in the class who are full time when teachers are job-sharing so that there is a consistent adult in the room (Tomsett, 2020).

What the school's objectives are, or which benefits they are trying to achieve from job-shares is important in determining the best compatibility of partners. There is no one-size-fits-all policy or set of rules that will work for everyone. In situations where the aim is to retain a member of staff, a key consideration is finding someone they can work well with but, as always, the most important factor is the impact on the pupils. There may be times when children, of all ages, would benefit from having two very different teachers with different skillsets or personalities. Resistance to job-shares often comes down to concerns about consistency, but there are times when the difference is the value in the arrangement. All children can have some time with a teacher they really connect with. In the case of job splits rather than true job-shares, the compatibility between partners might not matter so much, just the ability and skills to do their parts of the job.

Accountability

One of the questions that people often have about talent partnerships is how the accountability will work. There are concerns about who will be responsible if something goes wrong or where praise is deserved for excellent results or successes. Sharing a job does not halve the responsibility. Yes, job-sharers cannot be held responsible for the actions of another person, but there is an agreement and expectation in the contract that they will carry out and be accountable for their role. This may be something that requires thought and planning at the job design stage. For example, will one teacher be responsible for writing and reading and the other maths, or will they both be jointly responsible? Maybe one teacher will teach Themes 1 and 3 of the A Level course and the other Themes 2 and 4. Middle leaders might share responsibility or be designated a certain year group, phase or subject area. Senior leaders and headteachers might have some responsibilities designated solely to them and others that they work on together. Where responsibilities are shared, having a job-share partner does not make people less accountable. It should still be clear what they are responsible for and they should be held to account for that. In addition, job-sharers often feel additional accountability because of the duty they feel to perform well for their job-share partner.

Something which may help is being clear on which type of job-share is being set up. Capability Jane are an organisation who promote flexibility working across all sectors. They categorise job-shares into three types (Capability Jane, 2011):

- Job split: independent liability, each person has their own responsibilities
- Hybrid share: some shared and some divided responsibility
- Pure job-share: joint liability, both or all partners are responsible and accountable for all aspects of the role

Case study 7.2 Talent Partnership in Senior Roles, Claire Walker and Hannah Essex

Claire and Hannah were Joint Communications Directors for a number of years at Teach First and they talk about the additional layer of accountability that they feel as part of their partnership. They do not want to let each other down, and they seek ways to be more effective for themselves and each other. This drives them to do a better job more than the sole accountability of working in a traditional way would have done. Their role was not school based but, as senior leaders at Teach First and now as Co-Executive Directors of the British Chambers of Commerce, they know the importance of accountability at the top of an organisation, and they recognise and advocate the benefits of job-sharing at an executive level.

Recruitment

There are two elements to this, the first is considering how you recruit job-sharers to a post and the second is what you do if one talent partner leaves. The wider recruitment aspects are covered in more detail in Chapter 6 but, in terms of recruiting, when one talent partner leaves this may cause concern to school leaders worrying about if they would be able to recruit someone who was both looking for those part-time hours and compatible with the remaining talent partner. However, part-time posts are actually in high demand and data from TES say that mentioning flexible working in job adverts can actually increase the number of applicants substantially (TESGlobalCorp, 2017). If talent partnerships are common in your school, then staff moving on might provide opportunities for changes to staffing and existing talent partnerships, allowing others to increase their hours or change the combinations of job-share partners.

Advice for effective talent partnerships

As talent partnerships become more common in the education sector, we can better understand what makes them more effective and how schools can best set them up and support those in the education sector who are job-sharing. Generic advice for job-sharing is plentiful. For example, all jobs are available as job-share in the Civil Service and they provide guidance and advice for job-sharers in their 'Civil Service HR Guide to Job Sharing' (Civil Service, 2021).

Communication and collaboration within the talent partnership

Being clear with each other on expectations and communication between talent partners is crucial. The ideal situation is having proper, formal, paid time to catch up or hand over and to update each other. Being clear on expectations of each other is really important too. Having clear job roles and descriptions is a pre-requisite here. Working together and with line managers and subordinates, it is essential to make sure that responsibilities are clear and that nothing 'falls through the gaps'. A calendar or schedule mapping out daily, weekly, half termly, termly, annual tasks can be really useful for this – especially if it signposts relevant documents/materials for each task too. Using technology can aid this with shared access to the schedule as well as each others' calendars and linked documents. This also benefits succession and contingency planning, making the process much smoother if one talent partner is off work or leaves. It can make the replacement or cover arrangements much more efficient and successful. Online technology and software can be of huge benefit here too. We share all of our work and documents online which helps us to see the progress each other has made and easily share notes, information and tasks to be done. Having one shared e-mail account that both job-share partners have access to is really helpful, particularly if you share an entire role. You can monitor e-mails and issues coming through and see replies or drafts from the other person. People can easily contact you with any information or questions they have, and you can divide up tasks or actions. It also helps with how you are viewed from outside of the role: to all stakeholders, you are effectively the same person. Essentially the same service, commitment and responsibility regardless of who physically types a response to the e-mail.

Clear expectations and communication for others

A single e-mail address is again highly useful here. It means staff do not need to worry about which one of you to contact or remember who is working on which day and allows the talent partners to divide up any incoming queries or work appropriately. Email sign offs at the bottom of e-mails or automatic response notifications that can state individual working days and/or provide clarity for who the main contacts are and how the talent partnership works also provide clarity for those outside of the partnership. As an example email sign off, 'Jack is on site Monday and Tuesday, Jill is on site Wednesday and Thursday and both are in on Friday. If you have an emergency safeguarding issue please contact Jo on extension 1234'. Flagging can be colour-coded to assign e-mails to individuals within the talent partnership. A joint e-mail account can be used to review each other's draft e-mails and to provide synergy for external communication where required.

Regular review

Particularly when the talent partnership is a new set-up and/or the talent partners are not used to working in this way or with each other, it is really important to check in on how it is going and review the arrangements. Formal check in and review times laid out in advance of the talent partnership beginning can help to address any teething problems or smooth out processes that are not working well. Line managers and talent partners all need to be open, honest and reflective about this, but it helps to be positive as well. Do not be hard on yourself or your employees if it is not working out; there might be easy fixes to some of the issues and ways to move it forward. Like anything in life and schools, it may take time to get it working well and even if it is successful, it still needs regular review and tweaking to ensure it continues to produce the best results possible for staff and students. Consultation with those impacted by the working arrangements is crucial for this. Amy Gallo writing for the *Harvard Business Review* (Gallo, 2013) talked about the importance of not sitting on problems and not leaving anything unspoken as well as actively managing expectations and battling bias.

Case study 7.3 Shared Headship Network

The Shared Headship Network is an organisation which supports schools and their members to create shared leadership roles. They pair ambitious school leaders who aspire to headship based on values and experience. They represent a creative solution to the recruitment crisis in education and truly believe that two heads are better than one.

Some of the benefits they put forward of shared leadership and collaborative practice are as follows:

- Shared and therefore increased accountability from leaders for school staff and governors.
- Increased presence around school, for staff and students. More time for heads to observe lessons, circulate corridors, welcome parents and new students, lead assemblies and pop in to extra-curricular/form-time activities.
- Increased levels of experience and skills.
- Co-heads learn and reflect from each other, meaning leaders are more well rounded, empathetic and skilled in a variety of tasks.
- More flexibility – for schools and staff. Shared leadership makes a statement in a school. It champions ideas of flexibility and raises aspirations in staff who would otherwise feel limited by their personal commitments to progress to leadership.
- Increasing the number of young leaders and female leaders. 74 per cent of teachers are female, while 65 per cent of heads are female. This means there is an average of 1700 female teachers per year who could become heads but are discouraged from doing so because of the culture in education – the Shared Headship Network can change this!

Can talent partnerships work in all settings and roles?

One of the biggest concerns about talent partnerships we come across, is that they do not work in certain contexts or job roles. What follows is a list of examples of talent partnerships working in various types of school and role, at different leadership levels and in different settings.

Class teacher – Primary School, East Midlands

A Year 5 class at a primary school in East Midlands has two teachers who work in a talent partnership. One teacher works from Monday to Wednesday until the other teacher takes over for the rest of the week. The first teacher focuses on art and literacy, which are the subjects she is most passionate about. Then the children get a 'new' teacher mid-week who is energised and enthusiastic, ready to teach them. It also allows the school the opportunity to retain these two experienced, effective teachers who would not be available if the post was full time.

SENDCO – Reach Academy, Feltham

The Reach Academy Feltham is an all-through free school which opened in Feltham in the London Borough of Hounslow in 2012. Rather than having one person act as a SENDCO for the entire school from Early Years through to Sixth Form, they have three separate individuals sharing the role and specialising in particular Key Stages. This has allowed them to recruit and retain expert SENDCOs in the academy and they are able to focus on their areas of expertise as well as working together on ensuring effective transition and the sharing of good practice. Each member of staff works part time as SENDCOs allowing them to pursue other activities alongside the role. This might be classroom teaching, further education, their own caring responsibilities or other pursuits. Acting as a SENDCO for such a large range of ages, with such large numbers in each year group, would be a very difficult job for just one individual; separating the Key Stages and sharing the role makes sense for the school and the pupils, as well as for the staff members.

Senior Leadership – Saffron Walden County High School

Caroline Derbyshire, Executive Headteacher, CEO of Saffron Academy Trust, describes the leadership of Saffron Walden County High School's 650-student outstanding Sixth Form as an excellent example of the school's Flexible Working Policy applied to meet the needs of the organisation and its employees. Helen Cox and Amy Kennedy job-share the role as Co-Directors of Sixth Form. Helen plans to retire shortly and requested to become part-time to stage her retirement and build up her portfolio out of school interests. Amy was ambitious to increase her leadership role and influence in the school while managing the demands of her young family and a partner whose military career often leaves her as a single parent for periods of time. She applied to be Head of Sixth Form hoping that the school would accommodate a 0.8 PTE request. Helen and Amy work different days but overlap one day a week for the purpose of meetings and ease of communication. Helen appreciated the chance to ease into her retirement and said the arrangement made her feel valued after her years of service to the school. It enabled the school to retain two excellent colleagues, to build in a smooth succession model for the leadership of the Sixth Form and provided greater leadership capacity during a period of expansion. It was also good for morale. Staff feel valued and are proud to be part of a modern and forward-thinking organisation. Caroline says 'Happy, motivated and fulfilled staff provide a better experience for the students in the school'. This is evidenced through the exceptionally strong attainment and progress of the students in SWCHS Sixth Form. The Sixth Form retains an ALPS 2 grading, placing it among the best 2 per cent of Sixth Forms nationally.

Co-headteachers – Boxgrove Primary School, Surrey

Co-headteachers Alison Fitch and Rebecca Stacey talk about the fact that not only do they bring additional energy to the role, but they also have time to think, time to reflect and consider, and as a result, they do not have a constant threat of burnout hanging over them. It also reduces the sense of isolation; having someone to share problems with makes it easier to shoulder the great burden of being the headteacher. They are in it together and support each other. They also describe the benefits from the parents' point of view; having two options means that some families will prefer dealing with one over the other and it also helps spread the load too. As is often the case, the opportunity arose for them to job-share organically. An interim headship came up and neither of them wanted to take on a full-time post due to childcare, but as deputy and assistant head at the time, they had worked with each other for many years and made a strong case for a job-share. They used their experience of the school and the leadership team and proved it was a workable model.

Class teachers/middle leaders – Special School – Dorothy Goodman School

Rachel Barker and Simon Roadley share the Key Stage 4 class at their special needs school in Hinkley, Leicestershire. Rachel works Monday, Tuesdays, Wednesdays plus Friday morning and Simon works Wednesdays, Friday afternoon. They previously shared a class to allow for Simon to develop his specialist area of PE further in the school and to cover Rachel's leadership time. Following Rachel's flexible working request to reduce her hours to part time, the current arrangements are put in place. The arrangement enables them both to pursue leadership roles and whole school improvement initiatives.

The talent partnership works well for them because they have clear expectations and roles, for example Simon teaches Maths once a week and Rachel twice. Simon focuses on accreditation and Rachel works on core maths skills that support the accreditation. The flexibility of job-sharing means that they can pick up for each other at times when either of their whole school roles becomes more demanding. They are both experienced, effective teachers and are able to maintain consistency on core values and strategies. Despite having very different teaching styles, they have a shared ethos. Students experience a different way of working from multiple people, faces and voices in the classroom. This stops certain strategies being reliant on a particular teacher delivering them.

The class Teaching Assistant is a strong practitioner, which makes the transition between teachers much easier and keeps the consistency of approach as strong as possible. The TA acts as a really good bridge between Ms Barker and Mr Roadley and is able to fill in gaps in communication when they do inevitably occur.

Simon says "This has been the most effective job-share that I have been a part of (having also done this with several other teachers and classes). The shared ethos, respect and understanding that Rachel and I have has been the key to the success of the job-share as this consistency is hugely important in making it work".

Case study 7.4 Victoria Brooks and Kirsten Kennedy, Co-headteachers

We have included this story from co-headteachers Vicky Brooks and Kirsten Kennedy not just because we are so proud to have introduced them to each other through Flexible Teacher Talent, but because they both came to flexible working as a result of their personal circumstances, and wish to continue it as a progressive and valuable leadership model.

With valuable experience in education, and looking for ways to stay in leadership, Victoria Brooks and Kirsten Kennedy embarked upon their first co-headship role after we introduced them using our Twitter platform to find a suitable talent partner. They are both contracted to work 0.6, so the headteacher salary is paid for six days a week rather than five, but they are the entire leadership team and there are no assistant or deputy headteachers in their small primary school in Leicestershire.

Kirsten

I wanted to stay in schools after having my son and had thought about going back to teaching or lecturing: basically anything to stay in education, but I felt as though I had done a good job so far as a head, and I wanted to continue in school leadership. You know that it is still your name above the door even with a strong support network and strong assistant headteachers and I wanted something different now that I had my son. I was thinking about this during one of the four o'clock in the morning feeds and, a few weeks afterwards, I saw the ad on Twitter. Then we talked on the phone and it was like online dating because we got to know each other, but we did not actually meet in person until we had completed the interview and had started the job as co-headteachers.

We started looking at vacancies and that is where it gets a little bit complicated because, of course, everyone wants you to apply separately and I had been a headteacher before, so had a different experience level to Vicky. Some schools wanted me to apply on my own and I had to say that I was committed to us applying together. We looked through each other's applications so that we kind of matched up and so we almost appeared an obvious match on paper and then we have come to a trust which is quite innovative.

I think if we did not have the same values, it would be harder. It is quite like a marriage and any bust-ups, we deal with those privately and no one would have known. We have learnt a lot about our own personal traits. We cannot both take the lead on everything and we need to relinquish control and allow that. We have both come with our own experiences and ways of doing things, but in the end, the final product will be the best bits from both of us.

This is the most I have enjoyed headship. I have never been happier and being able to switch off and know that Vicky is there and capable as the headteacher on the days I am not there is wonderful. The only time we have to call is when there is a COVID bubble, which always happens on my day! It works for us to have an 'after bedtime meeting' to go through the day and catch up before the other of us takes over. Sometimes this is quite late but that works for us and equally, when we need a complete break we say so and will not contact each other.

The Trust are watching and waiting to see how it goes and they are pleasantly surprised with how well it is working. The parents seem to be very positive about it. It is still difficult for people to get their heads around it for a permanent model, rather than something we will do while we have small children.

Vicky

I had been at the same school since I was a student teacher and was now assistant headteacher. I had a very forward thinking headteacher who allowed me to come back three days per week after having my first child and I shared teaching Year 6 with the head. That headteacher left and I was deputy until an interim headteacher came in. I knew that the governors would not go for a co-headship and I felt really lost. I was looking for a way to stay in leadership. I followed Emma Turner and Flexible Teacher Talent and the Shared Headship Network on Twitter, so I got in touch to say 'Look can you throw this out there? I do not know if anyone else is out there and willing to go for it'. I got in touch with you in January, we interviewed in March and now we are coming up to one year in post. We're settling into our areas of expertise and share out responsibilities which match our expertise and interests.

We have phone calls in the evening on the days we do not work and we're nearly a year in. Going forward, we see it as a long-term thing. We want to continue as a co-headship, not just for this time in our lives.

Staff at our school have been very open to the model and we have worked really hard to convince the parents. We are conscious about being on the same page and that we are consistent. With Kirsten, I do not ever have to pretend to be anything that I am not and we are more relevant for the general parent population. The other headteachers in the area are inquisitive. We are advocating this as a model to keep good people and good women in leadership.

We are able to be flexible with our staff. We make decisions for teachers which suit their individual circumstances, and we give teachers and parents an opportunity to have meetings after school or after bedtime and that is a really welcome time slot which people appreciate.

It is a new leadership strategy and I want to champion women who are good at their jobs and want to continue their careers, as long as the children are happy. I bring the dog that gets you brownie points, but I also get called by Mrs Kennedy on a daily basis! I believe what they get is the best of both of us.

Final thoughts on talent partnerships in schools

Many of the schools we have seen who set up talent partnership arrangements do so initially to accommodate a request for flexible working from a current member of staff, but when it is seen positively and supported, schools often realise many unexpected benefits. Early on in this chapter we spoke about two heads being better than one, and commercial organisations already embrace the concept of talent partnerships and the benefits they bring, not just in terms of recruitment and retention but also in terms of productivity, innovation, staff wellbeing and diversity. The benefits of working together and sharing a role are huge for succession planning and development of staff, for sharing best practice, for making sensible decisions and coming up with new ideas, for managing staff workload and stress levels. Talent partnerships offer so much more than an opportunity to allow staff to work flexibly.

Summary

This chapter has described:

- How talent partnership arrangements can work in schools
- Practical advice and guidance for successfully managing talent partnerships in schools
- The benefits that can be gained from a more proactive and positive approach to talent partnerships in the education sector

References

Capabiltity Jane (2011). Job sharing at senior level: A guide for individuals. Available at: https://capabilityjane.com/wp-content/uploads/2018/05/CapabilityJane-Individual-Guide-to-Job-Sharing-at-Senior-Level.pdf (accessed 4 July 2021).

Civil Service (2021). Civil service HR guide to job sharing. Service.gov.uk. Available at: https://assets.publishing.service.gov.uk/government/uploads/system/uploads/attachment_data/file/406045/JobShareGuide260115FVnoDNs.pdf.

Folkman (2021). The confidence gap in men and women: How to overcome it. *Zenger Folkman*. Available at: https://zengerfolkman.com/articles/the-confidence-gap-in-men-and-women-how-to-overcome-it/ (accessed 2 July 2021).

Gallo, A. (2013). How to make a job sharing situation work. *Harvard Business Review*. Available at: https://hbr.org/2013/09/how-to-make-a-job-sharing-situation-work.

Gascoigne, C. and Kelliher, C. (2017). The transition to part-time: How professionals negotiate "reduced time and workload" i-deals and craft their jobs. *Human Relations*, 71(1), 103–125.

Lexico Dictionaries. Available at: https://Www.lexico.com/Definition/Job-Share.

Renn, C. (2020). Teacher wellbeing index 2020. *Education Support*. Available at: https://www.educationsupport.org.uk/resources/research-reports/teacher-wellbeing-index-2020.

TESGlobalCorp (2017). Flexible working recruitment insights. *TES*. Available at: https://www.slideshare.net/TESGlobalCorp/flexible-working-recruitment-insights (accessed 26 October 2020).

Tomsett, J. (2020). Is flexible working for teachers truly possible? *TES*. Available at: https://www.tes.com/magazine/article/flexible-working-teachers-truly-possible (accessed 2 July 2021).

TUC (2019). Workers in the UK put in more than £32 billion worth of unpaid overtime last year - TUC analysis. [online] www.tuc.org.uk. Available at: https://www.tuc.org.uk/news/workers-uk-put-more-ps32-billion-worth-unpaid-overtime-last-year-tuc-analysis (accessed 2 July 2021).

Sandberg, S. (2013). *Lean In: Women, Work, and the Will to Lead*. New York, NY: Alfred A. Knopf.

8

PART-TIME WORKING IN SCHOOLS

In this chapter we will:

- Explore the way part-time working can be organised in schools
- Describe best practice and considerations which will help to make part-time working successful
- Discuss ways to address some of the common challenges to having part-time staff

Introduction

Part-time arrangements are the most common form of flexible working that we think of and see in schools. The percentage of teachers working part-time has stayed steady in recent years (at around 22%), but it is still significantly lower than in the general population. Around 8.6% of male teachers work part-time, compared to 13% of men in the workforce nationally, and the difference is even greater for women: 26.4% of female teachers work part-time, compared to 42% of women in the workforce nationally (DfE, 2017). This is not just a problem for equality in the teaching workforce, it is also a factor in attracting and keeping high-quality teachers.

What does part-time look like in schools?

Part-time arrangements can take a wide variety of forms. Commonly we see part-time as 0.8 or 0.6 timetables translated into four or three days a week, respectively, but any proportion of working hours can be spread in any way across the week and may be worked either on site or remotely, offering a huge range of flexibility options for both schools and the individual.

Some examples of part-time arrangements

- Year 4 class teacher who works 0.6, three days a week. The class have specialist music, PE, art, languages and PPA cover provision on the other two days.
- Deputy headteacher works 0.9 and has every other Friday off school.
- Maths teacher works 0.5 with timetabled lessons five mornings a week.
- Economics teacher works 0.8 timetable across three days, with PPA and free periods all falling on the fourth day so only attends school three days a week.
- Key Stage 1 PPA cover teacher covers every teacher's PPA mornings and afternoons, working 60% of the week.
- History of Art teacher only required to teach one A Level class, five periods a week, so a specialist is hired to work a 0.35 timetable rather than hire a full-time art teacher with little experience or a full-time history of art teacher who needs to then to teach the rest of the week out of subject specialism.
- English teacher with chronic health condition works 0.8 across five days with late start each morning.

Making part-time working work in schools

There are a number of considerations which may help make part-time working arrangements more successful in schools, which we will explore in more detail.

Expectations

If expectations are pre-arranged, discussed and agreed, then there is less likely to be any disagreement or awkward discussion about them. Part-time staff are less of 'a pain' to manage if both the school and the employee are clear on the expectations and arrangements in place. If a discussion and negotiation occur every time a new query arises for each individual, then it can be time consuming and stressful for everyone involved. Part-time workers should not be made to feel like a nuisance for asking about these things; effective managers and leaders should have already thought about, and clearly communicated, how it will work.

Below are examples of conversations which should take place.

- Expectations for attendance to evening events
  - Should be pro rata and only in school or working days. Time off in lieu or overtime payments could be given if attended but staff should not be made to attend.
- Expectations for attendance to INSET or CPD days on non-working days
  - Again, part-time workers should not have to attend unpaid on non-working days or times. However, consideration should be made to how they will catch up on anything

missed and the importance of their in person attendance. Remote attendance or recording meetings are now much more viable options besides paying overtime.

- Communication expectations
    - on non-working days or times, both parties should be clear on how much, and through which mediums, flexible workers can be contacted, if at all, as well as how much and what types of work they can be expected to do.
- Timetables
    - Knowing how and when timetables for the following academic year will be decided is often a great help and reassurance for part-time staff. Waiting until September to have working days and timetable confirmed makes it impossible to manage other commitments like childcare, for which the part-time working has been requested.
- TLR payments and expectations
    - The government's guidance on the part-time TLR payments is that both payments and responsibilities should be pro rata if post-holders are part-time. No one should be expected to carry out the full duties of a post for only part of the pay. If completion of all the activities is required, then they should be remunerated appropriately. If payments are reduced, it should be made clear which duties are also reduced.
- CPD
    - Part-time workers are still entitled to, and want, development opportunities. They should not be excluded from training events or courses. Better use of remote learning technologies may allow them to catch up later with a recording or take part from home.
- Share of duties and tasks
    - Key stage or departmental planning responsibilities should be pro rata too. If each member of the team is expected to complete a 10-week scheme of learning, it is unfair to ask a 0.5 teacher to complete as much as a full-time teacher.

> *Actively supporting flexible working helps to retain people within the profession, particularly those who are experienced, and this involves providing professional learning and leadership opportunities for part-time workers.*
>
> Ruth Whymark, headteacher at The Vineyard School in Richmond upon Thames (Tomsett, 2020)

Communication

Many of the considerations mentioned in the previous section come down to clear communication and many of the potential barriers for part-time working can be negated with effective communication.

Here are some ideas which might help:

- E-mail footers
    - A note on an e-mail signature explaining working hours/days and expectations when not available can save a great deal of confusion and misunderstanding. This can also help with the next point on what to do or who else to contact if necessary.

- Clarity and understanding on appropriate communication
  - Do staff, parents and pupils know what to do if they cannot reach a member of staff? Is there an understanding of which items need urgent communication, which can wait and of the best medium for different messages? This is important for urgent messages relating to safeguarding but there are many messages which can and should wait. We have recently moved away from whole school e-mails and instead important, whole school messages are published once a week on Teams. This makes it less likely that part-time staff will 'miss' an important deadline e-mail or link.
- Use of meetings
  - Are they done virtually or in person? How do those who miss them for whatever reason catch up? Recording sessions can be very helpful for this and with the new technology we have all adapted to using in schools, it can be done relatively easily. Ideally, you do not want people having to spend lots of time catching up, but it is not always possible to plan to make sure everyone is included. It is important to look at what can be and is done in meetings versus what might be done by e-mail or online.

Case study 8.1 Putney High School

During lockdown, our SLT used PowerPoints with interactive links and sound recording explanations to share information with the whole staff rather than e-mails. They set out really clearly which events and deadlines were coming up, shared guidance and exemplars for reports and links to forms or surveys in clearly titled slides. An index on the first slide makes it easy to navigate and refer back to. It is sent at the same time every week so there is no need for lots of e-mails throughout the week or searching back through your inbox or Teams to find an attachment or information. It has made it so much easier for me to switch back into work mode and catch up on my school days and makes it much less likely that I will miss something when I am off site or busy. It is such a small but helpful change to have a central point to refer back to for all announcements, tasks and information as well as a vehicle to share examples of best practice and links to resources and opportunities. It makes communication and tasks simpler and clearer for everyone, not just part-time staff.

Clarity of communication will help the whole staff, not just part-time colleagues. Schools who actively seek to communicate effectively with staff can see many benefits for working relationships, workload and effectiveness. We explore here a number of reasons why.

- Better access to information reduces workload and makes life easier, the effort and difficulty of staying on board with initiatives and deadlines is lessened if details are clear and easy to find and refer back to.
- Better use of staff time – teachers are a school's most expensive and important resource, so using them wisely and minimising the time they spend on administration or in meetings is important, plus it supports their wellbeing and workload at the same time.

- It makes it easier to catch up if staff are absent for any reason. This has been particularly important during the COVID-19 lockdown, but there are always reasons that colleagues may miss briefings, e-mails or messages and the easier it is for them to catch up, the better for everyone.
- Reduces the burden of admin and much unnecessary communication – which saves time and improves efficiency.

Scheduling

When schedules are being drawn up for individual meetings or duties or other activities, it really helps to maximise the chance that part-time staff can fit it into their working week if this is done first for them. Part-time staff are in school for fewer days or times of the week, so they have fewer options in terms of scheduling. Staff who are in for the whole week have more scheduling options available.

Preferences

School leaders should not assume that everyone wants Monday and/or Friday off. It may be the case that colleagues would prefer shorter days or later starts or have particular days when they can arrange childcare. The type of flexibility required may also change, or not be as expected. Would primary staff prefer doing PPA cover or being a class teacher? Would secondary staff prefer to retain the same days/pattern for the next academic year for childcare purposes or are they flexible? Do not assume you know what staff want. Not everyone coming back from maternity leave wants to go part time: staff may wish to work more or fewer hours each year depending on their circumstances. Often flexibility is not required permanently and it may just be at times of transition or when health, caring or childcare needs become too demanding to allow for full-time work.

Remember you can use changes in preferences to give what Emma Turner, author of *Let's Talk About Flex*, refers to as 'elasticity' in the school organisation or timetable (Turner, 2020). If there is an extra GCSE French class or no one opting for A Level DT next year, then this might be matched with the desires of part-time staff wanting to work increased or reduced hours. This is beneficial in terms of being reactive and supportive to changing requirements of individuals but also of the school. This flexibility, or elasticity, can allow for lean, dynamic and cost-effective timetabling. It also limits the prevalence of secondary teachers having to teach out of their subject specialism. This is an advantage not just for students who will receive expert teaching but also in reducing workload for staff. Teaching outside of the subjects or phase you are trained and experienced in can be difficult and time consuming. In short, it is better for the wellbeing of staff and the learning of pupils: win-win.

However, be wary that these discussions around changes to hours and days can be difficult and anxiety filled for part-time staff. They may feel pressure from the school to work more or fewer hours than they want to and, especially where timetables or class teachers are not finalised until July or even September, staff can be very worried about their hours and days changing, particularly in relation to commitments or childcare arrangements. Leaders can help to reassure staff with clear timelines and processes and by being open to discussion and negotiation. Allow staff to make suggestions or raise concerns in the process of deciding the timetable. Best practice is to review flexible working requirements for all staff members annually while also being responsive to needs arising throughout the academic year.

Case study 8.2 John Tomsett, Huntington School

'At Huntington School, we don't buy into that. We openly encourage part-time working because we want to retain our best teachers. We have 112 teachers but only 86 full-time equivalent teachers (FTE). Our part-time teacher contracts range from 0.2 to 0.8 FTE. We have a number of job-shares.

Now, I am not going to claim this is easy. There are practical issues that ensure part-time working is effective. It's all in the curriculum planning and the timetabling. Sticking rigidly to a well-established timeline for completing the timetable is crucial' (Tomsett, 2020).

The school asks all staff in September if they would like flexibility for the following year. By February they have given them an indication of their likely hours for the next year which is then confirmed in May. This allows part-time staff to make decisions about things like childcare or changing jobs with plenty of notice while also allowing the school to be responsive to any changes in timetable or options. His staff are happy because they are dealt with in a sympathetic and considerate way and everyone understands that the needs of colleagues and the school have to be balanced.

They have a blanket policy of accepting all requests for flexible working because they want to keep great teachers. The way that Mike Bruce, the assistant head with responsibility for staffing and curriculum planning, arranges the timetable plans ensures that staff feel valued and listened to. He promotes face-to-face conversations over e-mail and that helps him to understand the nuances of people's needs and preferences (Tomsett, 2020).

Our advice for schools is to have a clear timeline in place for the timetabling and staffing process. Consult every member of staff each year to see how their needs and preferences have changed. This is a great way to maximise the use of staff's time and their wellbeing, and can also help the timetable to be leaner in terms of cost and more efficient and effective in terms of specialisation and deployment of staff. Staff will feel grateful and loyal because they are listened to and their needs are met, or at least seriously considered. It gives the timetabler a full picture of the hours and staff available for use while at the same time helping teachers and school leaders to plan and manage their working and personal lives. Leadership teams who offer the opportunity to discuss flexible working to all staff on a regular basis are often surprised by how small and relatively easy the requests that are made by staff are. They may not want or need to work part time at all and there may be other opportunities for flexibility that can be offered to them (More on the alternative types of flexibility in Chapter 4).

Timetables

The most common barrier for secondary schools in accepting flexible working is the timetable. Traditionally, it has been seen as the biggest blocker for enabling teachers to work part time but more and more schools are using creative timetabling to make the timetable work for both their pupils and staff. With a positive approach, effective timetabling software and flexibility from timetable and staff, it can work.

Case study 8.3 Chris Cooper, Co-Founder and UK CEO Edval Timetables

Part-time staff may be seen as an obstacle in schools – difficult and time-consuming to accommodate effectively within the timetable. Quite simply this is largely a falsehood. By rethinking the problem and identifying innovative solutions, part-time staff can be seen as a rich asset, not an obstacle.

Some of the benefits of part-time staff are that with reduced loads, they can actually be easier to schedule in some cases and they can be flexible, and may cover activities on their days off like class excursions or even classes, as a slightly dynamic on-demand workforce. Part-time staff loads are reduced, allowing more flexible arrangement of staffing, such as used to 'make up' a small deficiency, instead of hiring another more expensive full timer.

Edval wants to move away from timetabling being seen as an administrative task and instead for it to be used as a thought leadership tool. They argue that software and expertise such as theirs can transform the way that timetabling works. The processes, people and attitudes linked to timetabling tend to be stagnant and things are done the way they always have been. Improved algorithms and systems ameliorate the functionality at student level and the ease of accommodating flexible working practices.

Here is some advice for school leaders:

- Ask your staff what they want annually
- Know, and regularly review, your staff specialisms, abilities, flexibility and limits
- Don't be constrained by what you have always done
- Be open to making small, individual class or teacher changes outside of the main timetable
- Investigate job or class shares
- Consider staff loading holistically not just in terms of teaching hours
- Option blocks should be done as part of the timetable process not as an addition or add on
- Consider an external timetable audit
- Consider introducing alternative timetabling software

Empowering people who work flexibly to understand how timetables are constructed and what the constraints and issues are can help them to suggest solutions or be more flexible in their requests. Who is the timetabler usually? Been doing it for years? Open to flexible working or just finds it a pain? #WomenEd have facilitated training sessions empowering women and others to access the timetabling process. Timetabling is improved if the process is more collaborative. Timetabling is an innovative, strategic and dynamic process, not a static procedure.

Some tips for making a timetable work for the needs of all staff are to timetable part-time teachers first and to empower and involve staff, particularly middle leaders in coming up with their own creative suggestions and solutions that work for them and their teams. The timetable should not be completed in isolation by one member of the senior team.

Obviously, the priority for the timetable and the staffing of classes first and foremost will always be the efficacy of the timetable for the children, but it can, and should, work for the staff as well. Happier staff, part-time or full-time, with better timetables are more productive and will be better teachers.

Rooming

Lucy Flower in her *The Happy Leader* blog (Flower, 2020) talks about how part-time staff are always bottom of the list in planning for rooming and staff work space. This may be inevitable, but leaders can at least be sensitive to it. Apologise for how difficult room movements and lack of workspace might be. If there is one small room change that will make the difference to just one afternoon for a part-time member of staff, then a full-time member of staff might not mind moving for just that period. Again, consistency and effectiveness for the children will always be the first priority here, but there may be a way to manage it so that it works for everyone. What should be avoided is an attitude of 'you get what you are given and it is tough'. Even where it is not possible for part-time staff to have consistency in rooming, a bit of understanding and sympathy or just the recognition of the additional difficulty could go a long way to maintain goodwill.

The pro rata principle

If someone on a 0.6 contract is only getting paid 0.6, then they should only be teaching a 0.6 timetable and should only be doing 0.6 of directed time. But how does that work in practice? What is removed from their responsibilities? If every teacher in the Geography Department is asked to develop a series of lessons, is it fair that a 0.6 member of staff is asked to do the same amount of work as a full-time teacher who works, and is paid, nearly twice as much? They may be happy to do this or want to do it, but it is important not to expect it and to acknowledge that they are going over and above what is required. This also applies to attendance at parents' meetings or evening events, to CPD out of working hours, to meeting on days off and so on.

There are ways to work around this issue, but again it requires thought and planning rather than addressing it as it comes up which can lead to confusion, disagreement and inconsistency. Consider asking a colleague working a 0.4 timetable to just attend the lower school open evening and not the Sixth Form one, or ask them to attend both but with paid overtime or time off in lieu.

CPD

If a part-time teacher attends an external CPD course or INSET on their non-school day, again they should be paid for it and not expected to do it in addition to their paid working days. We do not ask full-time staff to work extra, unpaid days on top of their normal employment so we should not ask part-time staff to do it.

CPD commitments and expectations should also be pro rata. For example, if full-time staff select and attend three twilight training sessions from an annual programme on offer, part-time staff should have to sign up to only one or two depending on the hours they work. They can of course opt to do more voluntarily if they wish, but this should not be expected of them.

The same principle applies to performance management targets. The number of targets should be reduced for part-time staff: they work less and so should not have the same requirements as full-time staff.

Final thoughts on part-time working in schools

The guidance and ideas included in this chapter may seem daunting or hard work to implement, but really it comes down to treating teachers and leaders in schools as human beings. The rewards for a positive and proactive approach to part-time working are manifold. Staff will be motivated, committed and better able to manage the blend of their work and home life. This will result in less burnout and better retention, but also in happier, healthier teachers who are better able, and more enthusiastic, to do their jobs. It can reduce the need for having teachers work outside of their area of expertise and reduce their workload burden. In terms of recruitment and retention, it offers obvious benefits for increasing your talent pool and retaining experienced effective teachers and leaders. It is common for part-time teachers to give more to the school than they are paid for, working on days out of school, doing more than their pro rata hours or responsibilities – this makes them very good value for the school. In addition to these benefits, there are often many more in terms of diversity, reduced training burden and increased availability of coaches/mentors in school. Chapter 2 deals with the benefits in more detail, but making these arrangements work in the short term, will effectively result in longer-term gains for the school.

Summary

This chapter has described:

- How part-time work can be organised in schools
- Practical advice and guidance for successfully managing part-time teachers and school leaders
- The benefits that can be gained from a more proactive and positive approach to part-time working arrangements

References

DfE (2017). *Flexible Working in Schools: Guidance for Local Authorities, Maintained Schools, Academies and Free Schools*. Available at: https://assets.publishing.service.gov.uk/government/uploads/system/uploads/attachment_data/file/833799/DFE_Flex_Working_Guidance_2017_FINAL.pdf (accessed 18 November 2020).

Flower, L. (2020). *How to Support Part Time Colleagues*. Available at: https://thehappyleader.wordpress.com/2020/07/24/how-to-support-part-time-colleagues/ (accessed 18 November 2020).

Tomsett, J. (2020). *Is Flexible Working for Teachers Truly Possible?* tes. Available at: https://www.tes.com/magazine/article/flexible-working-teachers-truly-possible (last accessed 18 November 2020).

Turner, E. (2020). *Let's Talk About Flex: Flipping the Flexible Working Narrative for Education*. Woodbridge: John Catt.

9

OTHER ASPECTS OF FLEXIBLE WORKING IN EDUCATION

In this chapter we will:

- Look at the impact that the COVID-19 lockdown / pandemic may have on flexible working in schools
- Consider flexible working as a part of wider work towards teacher wellbeing and diversity in schools as workplaces
- Discuss how recent changes might impact the future and the need for change in the sector

Introduction

When we originally mapped out the plans for this book, we intended to use this chapter to talk about other bits and bobs linked to flexible working that have not been covered in previous chapters. From ideas like on-site crèches to what was happening in other sectors with flex, to wider issues relating to flexible working. But writing it during a time of great turbulence and change made it hard to ignore the all-consuming impact of the COVID-19 pandemic. As a result, much of this chapter focuses on that – the changes, the potential impact, the future beyond the strange and unanticipated years that 2020 and 2021 have been. It remains to be seen how the impact will eventually unfold, but the pandemic has led to such an upheaval, not just in our schools but also in our professional and personal lives, that it seems wrong not to include and examine it here.

A changing world

The COVID-19 pandemic has changed the world. One feature of 'the new normal' is the acceleration of flexible and hybrid working options available in many sectors. This has further exacerbated the gap between the opportunities to work flexibly for teachers and those in other workplaces. There was already a significant disparity in flexible working options between teaching and other sectors, but that gulf is now even greater. This will impact on recruitment and retention.

People are re-evaluating how they live their lives, what is important to them, where they live, what they do, how much time they spend with children and loved ones, their work–life balance, commuting, and so on. Will there be changes in how society sees parenting and caring responsibilities? Maybe it will be the case that more men and fathers will be sharing the responsibilities and mental load of running a household and caring for family members, having seen or shared the load more during lockdown. Conversely, it may be the case that we have stepped backwards in terms of equality of household duties and workplace roles. Many women were forced to put their careers on hold during the lockdowns to care for and support others or due to a lack of childcare options or healthcare support. We saw that 40% of women said their career had been set back or put on hold since the pandemic hit, and 41% of women have left or considered leaving the workforce (Morris, 2021). Failure to provide suitable flexible working options compounds the issues for working women and working mothers especially. Inflexibility limits childcare options and increases childcare costs. The United Kingdom already has the second most expensive childcare in the world (Browne-Swinbourne, 2021).

Some people have enjoyed home schooling so much that they now want to be teachers. Some teachers have found home schooling so beneficial for their own children that they want to reduce their hours teaching and their children's hours attending school and teach them themselves. Demand for tutoring and specialist teaching outside of schools is soaring and teachers are in demand outside of the classroom in ways they may not have been before. For many, the structure of our education system and our view of education as parents has really been called into question.

There may also be an influx of new potential teachers into the profession due to the economic position resulting from the pandemic. Such a large economic shock has resulted in a severe recession and many people losing their employment or their job security. NowTeach, a teacher training programme for career changers from other sectors, has seen a huge rise in applications, a 70% rise in applications a month between March and May 2020 and three times as many applications in October and November 2020 compared with the previous year (Hill, 2021). NFER data shows that teacher training applications are up by 42% (NFER, 2021). This is not sustainable or enough to cover the increased demand for teachers, but it is still encouraging. However, these new recruits, whether for economic or purely vocational reasons, may well be used to, or need, flexible working options if they are to enter and remain in our schools.

At the other end of the spectrum, the impact of the pandemic on teacher attrition is yet to be seen. The reasons why more teachers and school leaders might be experiencing burnout are many and varied. All employees, regardless of their role or career, have been at risk of greater stress and anxiety during the pandemic with people experiencing significantly more stress, anxiety and depression during and after the first national lockdown began. Women and young people are the most affected, according to a study led by University of Nottingham and King's College London (Jia et al., 2020). However, some problems have very specifically affected the teaching profession, whether it be headteachers setting up COVID-19 testing centres in their school halls, primary teachers simultaneously managing both physical and online learning while their schools were allegedly 'closed' or secondary Heads of Departments managing the administrative burden, workload and emotional pressure of the teacher assessed grades process for Year 11 and Year 13. The portrayal of teachers in the media as lazy and ungrateful and the rhetoric on catch-up and lost learning have not helped staff morale at what has already been a very difficult couple of years for the profession. Added to this, headteachers have faced the most extraordinary and unexpected challenges: the last-minute policy changes and lack of guidance from the government, the withdrawal of funding and broken promises on laptop delivery. So, we may be headed for a leadership crisis as heads and senior leaders retire early or move away from the sector to recover from the stress and difficulty of the impossible task of leading through the pandemic. Almost half of headteachers surveyed said they were considering leaving the profession after the pandemic (Weale, 2020). Those waiting in the wings to step up may no longer want the responsibility, the accountability, the pressure and the headaches they have seen burden their line managers.

Another change that seems here to stay is distance learning. As wonderful as this is for allowing flexible and remote CPD and opportunities to learn and develop, it also makes it easier for people to change careers. Training to become an educational psychologist or a speech and language therapist or something completely unrelated to teaching like a transcriptionist or a probation officer may have become more accessible and flexible options now that some or all of the training or qualifications can be done online. The increase in demand for tutoring services from official government schemes, individuals and schools has led to many pivoting their teaching away from schools and into online or in-person tutoring. A Facebook group called 'Exit the Classroom and Thrive' has boomed in members from its inception in October 2020 to more than 52.5k members in January 2022 (see www.facebook.com/groups/LifeAfterTeachingExitTheClassroomAndThrive). It is filled with examples of teachers who have left the classroom and gone on to other employment or opportunities.

The group also features many examples of so called 'toxic' schools. Workplaces with a them-vs-us ethos between classroom teachers and the senior leadership team, where bullying, inflexibility and toxic cultures force people out of, not just the school, but often the profession altogether. Of course, not all schools are run like this but the sheer number of stories on that group reporting anxiety, depression and desperation in relation to how they are treated at work shows this is a very real problem.

A better future

Surely it is time for schools to re-evaluate how they attract, retain and treat their staff. How do we get the most out of them? How do we develop them? How do we keep them in our schools and make sure our students are getting the best possible experience? In Kat Howard's book *Stop Talking About Wellbeing* (Howard, 2020), she describes numerous examples of ways that school leaders can genuinely improve the wellbeing of their staff. The overriding principle is not to waste time with token gestures like one-off cake treats or yoga classes but instead to truly consider the workload, work–life balance and individual motivations of each person who works in your school. Valuing them as individuals, ensuring they have sufficient resource and time to do their job, letting them get on with teaching and providing and encouraging effective professional development. One of the chapters is called 'People before procedures' and it contains a significant section on flexible working. Kat suggests we should re-assess how we approach the value of teachers in our schools and start viewing 'staff not by the hours they are present, but by the advantage of having them as part of the formation of a strong and consistent staff body' (Howard, 2020, p. 315).

Many changes have made teacher wellbeing even more important in recent years but there have also been adjustments to how we do things that may have made this more possible and easier to achieve. So much of the 'way we do things' has altered in dealing with the lockdowns and the pandemic. It has fundamentally changed how we operate as schools and shown that the seemingly impossible is possible. Many of our ways of working and school systems changed, sometimes almost overnight. Big changes in communication, meetings, physical interactions, presence on site, parents' evenings and how we deal with teacher absences and illness. The vast majority of teachers and school leaders at least partially worked from home for a significant period during the lockdowns. It worked. It had to work, it wasn't planned for and in many cases it was far from ideal, but ultimately it worked. Kester Brewin said there were 'feelings of slight shock and pleasant surprise: when, because of Covid, staff had been strongly encouraged to work more flexibly and not be on site all day every day, the sky had *not* actually fallen in' (Brewin, 2021).

It is important to recognise that what we saw was not true flexible working and it certainly was not flexible working at its best. In many cases, people were juggling illness, home schooling and caring responsibilities as well as all the worries and stresses of the pandemic. It was not pre-arranged, planned for or strategic, it was just a sticking plaster to make ends meet, a stopgap, a last-choice resort. Despite this, there were many benefits: reduced commuting times, more focused work in your own space and time, meetings were often better run with more thought put into agendas, technology was used for sharing workload and ideas, people could spend more time on their own interests or with their children or pets, there was more chance to relax or eat healthily or exercise or get out in the fresh air. Of course, for some people, the opposite of these things may have been true, but for those who were happier and more productive working in this way with more flexibility or working remotely, going back to the old ways and forgetting the positives that flexible working can provide would be a waste and a great shame.

Why we need change now

We already lagged behind other sectors in terms of flexible working, gender pay equality and retention and recruitment, but changes brought about by the pandemic may have made it even more urgent that we address these growing issues.

Teachers and staff in our schools may be suffering from so-called 'long-covid'. Defined as 'not recovering [for] several weeks or months following the start of symptoms that were suggestive of covid, whether you were tested or not' (Nabavi, 2020). School staff have been identified as being more likely to be suffering for long-covid than many others because of their extended exposure to others due to the nature of their work. A cross-party group of MPs, led by Liberal Democrat Layla Moran, backed by the British Medical Association and members of the House of Lords, want the government to follow the example of countries including Spain, France, Germany, Belgium and Denmark, and formally recognise COVID as an 'occupational disease' (BBC News, 2021). This would mean that employees and their dependents would be entitled to protection and compensation if they contracted the virus while working, as teachers may have.

These employees, these people, need support from the government and from their employers. One of the ways we may be able to support those suffering from long-covid in school is with a better offer of flexible working. This may only be temporary to ease their return to school or it may be longer term to support their ongoing needs, but it is imperative that we have polices to support them as is our duty of care to staff with health needs. The NASUWT wants 'more supportive sickness policies that recognise the complex and changing nature of long-covid symptoms, which can see teachers going through extended cycles of illness, leading to periods of intermittent absence over a long period' (Stewart, 2021). Offering the opportunity to work flexibly may make the difference to us retaining these teachers, otherwise they may be unable to work at all.

Another impact of the pandemic has been the widening of the gender pay gap. Gender pay gaps exist and persist where there are barriers to the progression of women into highly paid roles or industries. A proper flexible working offer for both women and men provides better opportunities for women to progress to the most senior roles in organisations, it lessens the motherhood penalty and allows better balance of caring responsibilities and work between parents of either gender. There has been a significant negative impact on gender equality in the workplace since the pandemic started. Research from the Fawcett Society suggests the pandemic has had a devastating effect on gender equality and the UK risks falling even further behind international comparators in terms of the gender pay gap. The reports states that 'Evidence suggests we face a reversal of progress in workplace equality and that we may be turning the clock back decades' (Fawcett Society, 2020). So, the imperative to act on ensuring women can progress to senior leadership in schools is greater now than it ever was. By allowing women and men to work flexibly we give them a much better shot at a genuine choice on how they balance work and caring responsibilities. Allowing career progression for those working flexibly creates better diversity and gender balance in school leadership, which in turn leads to decision-making which is more balanced, representative and better meets the needs of school staff teams and the children they serve. Traditional ways of working have always created a glass ceiling for women, but the pandemic seems to have set this back even further so offering flexible working is more important than ever.

Given the potential impact on staff leaving and joining the profession, we are going to see greater staff turnover and a requirement for effective induction of new staff. Some trainee teachers coming into the profession are going to need more help. They had less time in schools with real pupils as part of their training, it has not been a normal couple of years and many of them will have had a very different training experience to the norm. They will need help from experienced and effective colleagues, as may those changing careers or coming into teaching for unexpected reasons and with families or other responsibilities to manage around their training. We will need to have experienced and effective people in post to settle in and grow this new generation of teachers which may mean allowing our current workforce more flexibility to keep them around. Many of these new recruits may also be used to, or need, flexibility in their working arrangements. If we wish to capitalise on this new influx of trainees and turn them into teachers who stay in our schools, then we must do a better job of accommodating their needs and meeting their expectations.

It is not just our teachers and staff teams that have been affected by the pandemic, it is also our pupils. Educational disadvantage has grown. Pandemic learning loss has undone up to two-thirds of disadvantage gap progress (Carr, 2021). Much of the progress that has been made in years gone by in terms of improving outcomes for those from the most challenging backgrounds and increasing social mobility has been lost during the lockdowns and interrupted schooling. The gulf between the haves and have-nots was exemplified in access to computers and broadband during online schooling but also highlighted how many children have insufficient available space, nutrition or support available to work at home. In addition, we saw that global majority (BAME) people and those from low-income families were more likely to contract and suffer from COVID-19. At the same time, many support services and mental health provision were stripped back, and the economic situation plunged even more households into poverty. So, it is now more important than ever to get good people in front of our children, especially the most disadvantaged, and to keep them there. That means attracting, retaining and developing not just enough teachers but also the best teachers. Over a school year, pupils from disadvantaged backgrounds gain 1.5 years' worth of learning with very effective teachers, compared with 0.5 years with poorly performing teachers (Sutton Trust, 2011). Suitable flexible working options is one way to ensure the profession is attractive and accessible to the best teachers.

Human resources

Schools are built on people. As an industry we provide a service which is highly labour-intensive. Our teachers and support staff are our main and most important resource. If we want to get the most out of them then we need to look after them. Regardless of the impacts of the pandemic, looking after school staff is important not just because they are humans, people who need and deserve to be treated with respect and have their legal rights upheld as employees and individuals, but also because getting more from your resources in our sector means better outcomes for our pupils. Looking after your staff is not just something that you have to do legally or something that would be a nice extra perk for them, it has the potential to make them better workers, more efficient, more productive.

Many schools do not have specialist human resources managers like businesses do. They do not have experts to write policies and devise ways to make staff happier and more able to do their jobs. Complex and important decisions about job design, flexible working policies, workloads, succession planning often fall to the headteacher or other senior leaders. Even if they are outstanding teachers and inspirational and effective leaders, they may not have any experience or idea about these complex personnel issues. However, doing this well is vital to the success of the organisation. There is external help available. Since 2018, the CIPD have had an active campaign to get trained HR people to join governing bodies and MAT boards. The CIPD has links with Inspiring Governance to help match HR professionals with governor vacancies in their local schools so contact your local branch. Other sources of support are local firms with large HR departments looking to use their corporate social responsibility, pooling with other local schools to share the expertise of an HR professional, or looking to recruit an HR professional part-time or on a consultancy basis. Getting and keeping the best staff for the needs of your pupils and making sure that they can do their jobs to the best of their abilities is at the core of running a successful school. Where the ultimate aim of the education sector is to do the best we can for the children in our care, the importance of looking after our staff cannot be neglected or ignored.

Many of us are uncomfortable with, or unused to, the idea of schools being businesses or organisations, but they are. Schools are workplaces. The data show that the school workforce is predominantly female, 75% of classroom teachers and 67% of headteachers (DfE, 2021). Just under half of teachers have their own children who are under the age of 18 (Teacher Tapp, 2017). So as workplaces we need to be conscious of these facts. Founder of the Maternity Teacher Paternity Teacher Project, Emma Sheppard, talks about the importance of schools being family friendly and how much sense that makes in terms of also being life friendly. In an article on their website Hayley Dunn, a school business manager, says, 'Schools with family friendly cultures and policies, make it easier for their employees to more easily balance work and life; in order to fulfil their obligations' (Dunn, 2017). This does not just apply to parents, but all employees. Flexibility for appointments or events, sensible meeting and parents' evenings schedules and requirements, clear and manageable workloads – it is not just parents this will help. The wider impact on staff morale and productivity may be even greater than first considered.

Summary

This chapter has described:

- How the pandemic may have positively and negatively impacted flexible working in the education sector
- The wider importance of flexible working for staff wellbeing
- The idea of schools as workplaces where maximising output requires effective use of resources

References

BBC News (2021). *Long Covid: MPs Call for Compensation for Key Workers*. BBC News, 18 February (online). Available at: https://www.bbc.co.uk/news/uk-politics-56090826 (accessed 22 June 2021).

Brewin, K. (2021). *What If "Flexible Working" Meant Leaving School Early?* Tes (online). Available at: https://www.tes.com/news/what-if-flexible-working-meant-leaving-school-early (accessed 22 June 2021).

Browne-Swinbourne, J. (2021). *Grazia, The Juggle and Pregnant Then Screwed Call Government for Childcare Sector Reform*. ppa.co.uk (online). Available at: https://www.ppa.co.uk/article/grazia-the-juggle-and-pregnant-then-screwed-call-government-for-childcare-sector-reform# (accessed 22 June 2021).

Carr, J. (2021). *Report: Pandemic Learning Loss Has Undone Disadvantage Gap Progress*. Schools Week(online). Available at: https://schoolsweek.co.uk/pandemic-learning-loss-has-undone-up-to-two-thirds-of-disadvantage-gap-progress/ (accessed 22 June 2021).

DfE (2021). *School Workforce in England: November 2020*. GOV.UK (online). Available at: https://www.gov.uk/government/statistics/school-workforce-in-england-november-2020 (accessed 22 June 2021).

Dunn, H. (2017). *Family Friendly Schools*. MTPT.ORG.UK (online). Available at: https://www.mtpt.org.uk/family-friendly-schools/family-friendly-schools/ (accessed 22 June 2021).

Fawcett Society (2020). *The Coronavirus Crossroads Equal Pay Day 2020 Report* (online). Available at: https://www.fawcettsociety.org.uk/Handlers/Download.ashx?IDMF=dbe15227-4c02-4102-bbf2-dce0b415e729

Hill, A. (2021). *From Finance Chief to Childminder: How Home Schooling Has Inspired New Careers*. The Guardian (online). Available at: https://www.theguardian.com/education/2021/mar/28/from-finance-chief-to-childminder-how-home-schooling-has-inspired-new-careers?fbclid=IwAR0dTEFahhG79CRdRAWdNGMwWry7D29bXn_rHMf1As2zoqtZRKkGjhabrZY (accessed 22 June 2021).

Howard, K. (2020). *Stop Talking About Wellbeing: A Pragmatic Approach to Teacher Workload*. Woodbridge: John Catt Educational.

Jia, R., Ayling, K., Chalder, T., Massey, A., Broadbent, E., Coupland, C. and Vedhara, K. (2020). Mental health in the UK during the COVID-19 pandemic: cross-sectional analyses from a community cohort study. *BMJ Open* (online), 10(9), e040620. Available at: https://bmjopen.bmj.com/content/10/9/e040620

Morris, N. (2021). *"Entitlement gap" in the Workplace Is Holding Women's Careers Back, Finds Study*. Metro (online). Available at: https://metro.co.uk/2021/03/01/entitlement-gap-in-the-workplace-is-holding-womens-careers-back-14163104/ (accessed 22 June 2021).

Nabavi, N. (2020). Long COVID: How to define it and how to manage it. *BMJ* (online) 370, m3489. Available at: https://www.bmj.com/content/370/bmj.m3489

NFER (2021). *Teacher Training Applications Up by 42 Percent*. NFER (online). Available at: https://www.nfer.ac.uk/news-events/nfer-blogs/teacher-training-applications-up-by-42-percent/

Stewart, W. (2021). *Fears Long COVID Is a "Ticking Time-Bomb" for Teachers*. Tes (online). Available at: https://www.tes.com/news/fears-long-covid-ticking-time-bomb-teachers (accessed 22 June 2021).

Sutton Trust (2011). *Improving the Impact of Teachers on Pupil Achievement in the UK -Interim Findings* (online). Available at: https://www.suttontrust.com/wp-content/uploads/2011/09/2teachers-impact-report-final.pdf (accessed 22 June 2021).

Teacher Tapp (2017). *How Many Teachers Are Also Parents?* Teacher Tapp : Ask · Answer · Learn (online). Available at: https://teachertapp.co.uk/many-teachers-also-parents/ (accessed 22 June 2021).

Weale, S. (2020). *Exodus of Exhausted Headteachers Predicted in England after Pandemic*. The Guardian (online). Available at: https://www.theguardian.com/education/2020/nov/18/exodus-of-exhausted-headteachers-predicted-in-england-after-pandemic

10

FINAL THOUGHTS

In this chapter we will:

- Reiterate the importance of flexible working in the education sector.
- Summarise our key recommendations on flexible working for schools.
- Review our key recommendations for individuals who want to work flexibly.

Introduction

It has been an interesting time to be advocating for flexible working. When we first met, we were frustrated by our own personal circumstances and by the workplace lottery which seemed to exist in terms of flexibility offered in schools. Organisations such as #WomenEd and The MTPT Project were addressing the detrimental impact for women of the lack of flexible leadership opportunities available and helping them to make the most of any career break they took for childcare. We read everything there was to read, spoke to anyone who would listen, and trialled a number of workshops and training opportunities which helped us to gauge what was most useful for schools and individuals in changing this landscape for flexible working in the education sector. Certain themes kept coming up and we used these to help us create resources and advice culminating in the content of this book. We want to stress again that as a sector, we are far behind. We understand that this is dictated by the nature of teaching which determines when and where we work, but.... but we still know the sector can do better.

There seems to be a disparity between the viewpoints of teachers and leaders on flexible working. In effective schools, this is almost invisible and staff work purposefully together to achieve their goals. When it comes to flexibility, the reactive model of individual requests means that teachers are at the mercy of the opinion and expertise of their leaders and particularly their headteacher. This can create a wedge between teachers and leaders when the clumsy mishandling of a flexible working request means that the profession loses staff who would have been catered for differently by a leader with a different set of experiences. We want to share this knowledge so that everyone is better informed, and can make better decisions based on their own setting. The education sector is rightfully concerned with the wellbeing of children in our care and what we can do to help. This does not always include sharing our model of how to manage and balance work and life. The martyr teacher staying up until all hours, rushing from work to home, never having time for their own interests is not a great model for our students. A little flexibility would go a long way to demonstrating that staff are trusted and empowering them to manage their time and resources more effectively.

The need for change

As a female-dominated profession, the impact of poor flexible working opportunities on the gender balance at leadership level and the lack of representation and progression of women matters even more than in other sectors. If our children's first experience of a community is their primary school where almost all of their teachers are female except the headteacher, who is a man, we are shaping their earliest ideas about who deserves to be in the 'top jobs'.

Early on, we recognised that the people working in this space often looked like us (white, cis-gender, able-bodied), so we sought out a wider range of voices. Part-time working is the most traditionally offered method of flexible working, but it is not necessarily the most inclusive model. Working part time as 'just' a classroom teacher relies on a two-salary household so it is a privilege. Fighting for flexibility demonstrates that we have time and energy because we are not already exhausted from fighting for other types of equity. Schools which do offer flexible postholder roles (TLR, SLT, headteachers), are more inclusive because they allow anyone to reduce their hours while avoiding salary sacrifice. Those schools are not asking single parents, (or any parents), to choose between their own children and the children they teach. Those schools are supporting carers who live with and care for both their parents and their own children. Those schools allow everyone to request elements of flexibility without feeling like they are rocking the boat or ruining their chances of future promotion and career progression.

We began to consider whether lack of flexible working not only limits career progression for those already in the education sector but sector, but also acts as a barrier to groups who have never been able to consider it. We know that flexible working will not solve all the sector's recruitment problems, but it does seem to solve many in a sector which is facing a recruitment crisis and haemorrhaging talent. We want to recruit and retain the most effective teachers in the classroom. This means attracting people who represent the student body and ensuring that they are able to remain in a profession which is almost 100% service user facing throughout their lives. We know that not everyone will want to work flexibly all of the time, but almost all teachers and leaders will need a degree of flexibility at some point in their career.

The time for change

Managing schools during a global pandemic with working conditions which none of us had ever experienced has been a time for school leaders to prove how incredibly adaptable and forward-thinking they are. It has demonstrated the lengths that staff will go to for their pupils and how much the relationships built in the classroom have an impact on the motivation and progress of students left to their own devices. COVID-19 was not a dress rehearsal for flexible working. However, the initial lockdown from March 2020 to July 2020 did allow for almost all teachers to experience a kind of autonomy in their workload and provided CPD opportunities which might not have been possible previously. Of course, many were unable to 'enjoy' this autonomy and expedited CPD as such, but there it was. Some elements which had been perceived as barriers to flexible working for so long just fell away and that is something we really want to hold onto moving forwards. There is more detail on the impact of COVID in Chapter 9, but the key learning about assumptions and possibilities for flexible working are as follows:

- Presenteeism does not equal commitment – staff do not have to be present all the time in order to live the values of the school and to have a positive impact on the pupils they serve.
- Remote meetings are possible and sometimes preferable.
- Whole staff CPD can be replaced with more bespoke, self-directed CPD which adds value to the students in a teacher's care. Trusting teachers to pursue a subject of interest to them and measure the impact of that in their classroom is a sensible way forward.
- Administration tasks can often be completed more effectively and uninterrupted off site.
- Avoiding the busiest commute time at the start or end of the day can have a huge impact on the wellbeing of individuals as well as lengthening the productive time in their day.

The DfE have been discussing options for flexible working and as we go to print, they are piloting financial investment in a regional project of Flexible Working Ambassador Schools (FWAS), and they have enlisted Timewise to work closely with the sector. We are always pleased when larger companies with bigger budgets and more experience echo what we know anecdotally: these projects serve to amplify our messages about the benefits of flexible working in education. Regional DfE funding and the employment of a market leader in Timewise is promising for both schools and individuals. Find out how to get involved in the project by approaching your regional FWAS and attending training webinars and workshops.

A school like mine

We have had the pleasure of meeting an amazing network of people who are often pushing for change and improvement on their own and while they are tired and vulnerable. We love to share stories about when things go well. We know that other settings learn from these stories and feel better able to implement change when they can see it happening in 'a school like mine'. We want to gather a large enough data set so that we can put schools in touch with others who are similar to them. Success of the London Challenge and now Challenge Partners model of school improvement demonstrates how well the sector responds to case studies which mirror schools in their context or 'family'. If you know you are going to make changes, please do make sure that you sign up on our website, so that we can begin to audit valuable data and use it to help shape changes which are necessary in a sector that we love.

There is no one-size-fits-all approach to flexible working in schools. The benefits, challenges, possibilities and barriers are all highly dependent on your school context, what can be achieved with flexible working, the benefits for your school, how it can address your difficulties; this will all depend on your school's individual characteristics, circumstances and people. For example, if you are an urban complex inner-city comprehensive school struggling to recruit and retain middle and senior leaders, then your needs and objectives in utilising flexible working will be very different to what they would be if you were a tiny village primary school. The types of flexible working that you can offer and that will work and the benefits it may bring are not homogenous. School leaders should see flexible working as a tool, as a strategic weapon they can deploy to solve their specific problems and to drive forward the development of their schools. The benefits reach far beyond those for the individual working flexibly. Flexible working can help you to deliver an appropriate and effective curriculum to ever-changing cohorts of children. Schools need to be more fluid and flexible in their staffing in order to be responsive and dynamic in their curriculum and provision.

Key recommendations for individuals

Where a reactive model still exists, requesting flexible working arrangements is incumbent upon a handful of often the most vulnerable members of staff making a flexible working request. You might be one of these people, so make sure you have considered the following in advance of making an application:

- You have a legal right to request flexible working as long as you:

  have worked continuously as an employee of the company for the last 26 weeks
  have not made a request to work flexibly under this right during the past 12 months.

- The wider sector is supportive of the idea of flexible working in schools. The DfE, OFSTED, the NAHT and other unions, and the NGA all support the adoption of flexible working practice to allow for the best use of the school workforce and to attract and retain high-quality staff.
- Consider what your role entails, how it can be broken down and who might benefit from sharing the responsibility of your role when you are not on site.
- Promote the positive impact of the new working pattern on your employer and colleagues as well as the benefits for you as an individual.
- Provide solutions for how your employer can best accommodate your new working pattern. Being flexible here and bringing several suggestions about the type of flexible working will really help your SLT come to a decision. Also, be open to suggestions that they make.
- Consider whether the flexible working arrangement is a temporary transition, or a more permanent arrangement as this may affect whether you have to make a formal flexible working request.
- Find examples of your post being done successfully in a flexible way in another educational setting, ideally one in a context similar to yours.
- Do not be ashamed of making a request for working flexibly. Be proud of pushing for better, fairer working arrangements for yourself and those who come after you. Be a role model and show others it can be done.

School business leader Hilary Goldsmith speaks about the need for teachers and those who work in our schools to speak out when things are not working. She says that change will only happen when real practitioners are brave enough to say something and to work together to offer solutions (Featherstone and Porritt, 2021). We will keep pushing for system-level change in the education sector and collaborating with others such as The MTPT Project, WomenEd, the Shared Headship Network, Emma Turner and the Department for Education, but real change will happen when teachers and leaders really see flexibility working successfully in their schools.

Key recommendations for schools

We advocate a proactive model where schools consult all their staff about their working requirements annually. Context is key and so leaders should think carefully about how flexible working aligns with the vision and values of the school. For examples of what this might look like, read Chapter 4.

The ideal process should be as follows:

1. Align commitment to types of flexibility with the priorities of your organisation.
2. Audit key data (cover, absence, cost of recruitment, retention of vulnerable groups), which you hope will be positively impacted by introducing more flexible working practices.
3. Ask each staff member annually how they would like to work.
4. Decide whether to offer specific contract types, or individually tailored contracts based on the needs of the school and staff body.
5. Trial, review and refine.

Suggested timing for this model requires debate and decision-making about how flexibility fits with the organisation in the summer or at the very start of the Autumn Term. In secondary schools, we suggest a questionnaire or one-to-one interview session for all staff by November, then a new proposed timetable ready for consultation in February which leaves time for advertising any new posts ready for September.

We are aware that in some settings, a whole school approach will take longer to implement than others. In these cases, there are elements of flexibility which can be introduced without an arduous amount of planning and preparation. We recommend starting with these, auditing key data which you hope to see improve and then reviewing. These ideas help to demonstrate trust to staff who then feel empowered and are likely to reward you with loyalty.

- Streamline your communication to all staff: one platform, once a week. Remote, recorded or written rather than in person.
- Consider your core hours for staff. Is there a stigma to staff leaving the site with the children if they have no other commitments? Why? Leadership can help to lose this stigma by setting an example and leaving early one day per week.
- Aside from compulsory Safeguarding, CPD should be bespoke and relevant to each individual teacher. If you hold regular (weekly) CPD for all staff to attend together, consider its purpose and find other ways for staff to develop individually.
- Talk to your staff and ask what they want. You will be pleasantly surprised.
- If you currently have a blanket ban on TLR or SLT positions being done part time, consider how inclusive this makes your school and your leadership team. Think more flexibly about how some of these roles might benefit from having more than one person responsible.
- Consider including a reference to flexible working arrangements in all of your job adverts. Conduct a blind process where you go through the interview process to choose the best person for the job and then allow them to negotiate flexibility if required.
- Start with the positive mindset of 'what can we do to facilitate this' rather than 'we cannot do this'.

It is time to move away from the assumptions and perceived barriers for teachers and school leaders working flexibly. Frances Ashton explains that 'lazy stereotypes' about part-time teachers perpetuate the idea that they are a nightmare to timetable, avoid CPD and are less ambitious (Porritt and Featherstone, 2019). There are barriers for schools in introducing flexible working. The biggest concern for primary schools is consistency for the children and avoiding confusion for the parents; for secondary schools it is the timetabling and split classes. As discussed, these barriers are based on assumptions and myths. Experienced co-headteachers Emma Turner and Claire Mitchell describe how, at the start of their journey together, there were many questions about the set up that they could not answer. There were some solutions that did not reveal themselves until they tested it out and found their way (Porritt and Featherstone, 2019). Taking risks and trusting people is the only way that schools can really move forward and change for the better. In these times of great uncertainty and turbulence it may be difficult for headteachers to change their ways of working: the added risk is unwelcome and there is no time or headspace to properly consider a shift to more flexible working. But if not now, when?

A call to action

This is a call to action. You are now better equipped to help change a sector which drastically needs updating in terms of its practices if it is to have a hope of rivalling others. We need to be kinder and more humane to all our colleagues, regardless of where they are working and who they are working for. Ask, try, review, revise and let us know how you get on. Together, we have the power to flex education.

Summary

This chapter has described:

- The importance of flexible working in schools
- What individuals can do to promote flexible working in the education sector
- How school leaders can change their mindset to capitlise on the opportunities of flexible working in their specific school contexts

References

Porritt, V. and Featherstone, K. (eds) (2019). *10% braver*. London: Corwin.
Featherstone, K. and Porritt, V. (eds) (2021). *Being 10% braver*. London: Corwin.

INDEX